Historical Association Studies

Gandhi
Against the Tide

Historical Association Studies
General Editors: Roger Mettam and James Shields

Gandhi

Against the Tide

ANTONY COPLEY

Basil Blackwell

To Raman and Rajeena
and to my students

First published 1987

Basil Blackwell Ltd
108 Cowley Road, Oxford OX4 1JF, UK

Basil Blackwell Inc.
432 Park Avenue South, Suite 1503
New York, NY 10016, USA

British Library Cataloguing in Publication Data

Copley, Antony
    Gandhi.——(Historical Association studies)
    1. Gandhi, M. K. 2. Statesmen——India——
    Biography
    I. Title   II. Series
    954.03'5'0924 DS481.G3
    ISBN 0-631-14514-1

Library of Congress Cataloging in Publication Data

Copley, A. R. H. (Antony R. H.), 1937–
    Gandhi.
    (Historical Association studies)
    Bibliography: p.
    Includes index.
    1. Gandhi, Mahatma, 1869–1948. 2. India——History——
    20th century. 3. Statesmen——India——Biography.
    4. Nationalists——India——Biography. I. Title.
    II Series.
    DS481.G3C59 1986 954.03'5'0924 [B] 86-19276
    ISBN 0-631-14514-1 (pbk.)

Typeset by Photo-Graphics, Honiton, Devon
Printed in Great Britain by Whitstable Litho Ltd, Whitstable, Kent

Contents

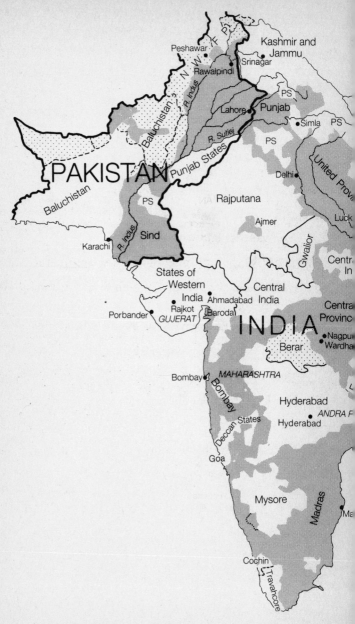

The Indian sub-continent at independence, 1947
Source: H. V. Hodson, *The Great Divide* (Hutchinson, 1969).

NEPAL

BHUTAN

R. Brahmaputra

Shillong•

Assam

•*hares*

•*R. Ganges*

•Patna

•*bad*

Bihar

PAKISTAN

Dacca• ES

Manipur

Bengal

•Calcutta

astern

States

Orissa

•Cuttack

Orissa

────── Boundaries between
         India and Pakistan

────── International Province or State
 ...... of Provincial Status Boundaries

  British India and
         Leased Territories

         Indian States

         Tribal Areas

Italic names denote
regions designated later.

PS = Punjab   NWFP = North West   ES = Eastern
     States   Federal   States
                            Province

1 Formative Influences: Ahimsa and Satya or non-violence and truth

If I were to draw up a short list of the most influential social and political thinkers in the twentieth century, few would quarrel with a choice of Marx, Lenin, Mao Tse-tung and Gandhi. Yet Gandhi is very much the odd man out in such company; it would be more accurate to see him as their antagonist than as a fellow thinker. Their materialism was wholly at variance with his spiritual concerns, however pragmatic we might deem these to be. Indeed, it was not until his last period of detention at Poona during the Second World War that Gandhi undertook any serious reading of Marx's writings. In saying this, however, we must not overlook one crucial convergence in their thought: they all laid as much stress on means as on ends, paying especial attention to *how* to bring about change. It is this element in Gandhi's thought that differentiates him from a whole cluster of earlier utopian socialists, men whose vision of a worldly paradise he shared but who lacked his visionary sense that it was as important to formalize the means of change as it was the ends. Gandhi is altogether far more attractive in his handling of this debate than Marx, Lenin and Mao. Theirs was an unscrupulous, ruthless, Machiavellian acceptance that the ends justified the means; a tolerance of the brutishness and violence of power-politics. Gandhi possessed an acute moral awareness that means would colour ends and that only just, non-violent means would lead to a just and harmonious society: 'the means may be likened to a seed, the end to a tree; and there is just the same inviolable connection between the means and the end as there is between the seed and the tree' (Gandhi, 1963, p. 43). It is that optimism and that endlessly argued idea which probably make Gandhi so attractive and so relevant a figure to the world of today.

1

How to explain Gandhi, the man known as the Mahatma, or 'great soul'? Wherein lay the origins of so charismatic a personality and so persuasive a mind? At the outset we must look, if briefly, at those family and intellectual circumstances that helped to shape the young Gandhi. Not that any exploration of such formative influences can explain the originality of a man of his stature: in the end, the man makes himself.

On the one hand, we must look at Gandhi's family background, at the relationship between himself and his parents as well as at his own role as husband and father. This will entail paying some attention to psychoanalytical explanations. Here Erik Erikson's *Gandhi's Truth* (1970) is one of the most important studies in recent Gandhi historiography, and some appraisal of his findings, however critical, should find their place in this study.

On the other hand, we must look at those intellectual and spiritual antecedents that contributed to the making of Gandhi's distinctive philosophy of non-violence, although one has to deal with particularly difficult material in order to understand his intellectual make-up. Gandhi's story has become part of a broader inquiry among Indian intellectuals into questions of identity; questions as to whether they should draw their ideas predominantly from the East or from the West. Indian intellectuals, in the colonial period, found themselves in a cross-fire of European and Indian ideas, and Gandhi was no exception. He had to pick and choose and fashion some identity of his own. Religion, however, had a deeper influence on Gandhi than as a mere source of ideas, and it will become clear that Indian religions, especially Jainism (Indian words and concepts with which the reader may be unfamiliar are explained in the Glossary), were a crucial factor in his spiritual growth. Historians have now put behind them the essentially arrogant view of earlier Western interpreters, which was that the choice for Indian intellectuals lay between a modernizing West and a traditional India. The quest for identity is now studied through a more sophisticated model in which the traditionalist is seen as a modernizer with Indian intellectuals now seen as seeking the source of modernity within their own traditions. In many ways this is a model that works well for Gandhi, but we still have to explore the extent of the influence of Western writers on his ideas and the degree to which he was to assume an Indian and more specifically a Hindu identity.

Gandhi was in no sense an academic. It would be quite wrong to ascribe to him any formal or structured philosophy; it is difficult to know just how systematic or random a reader he was. He had a prolonged formal education, culminating with his qualification as a lawyer, but he received little formal instruction in those questions with which he became increasingly concerned, questions of moral and political philosophy, and of religion. It was imprisonment that provided Gandhi with one of the best opportunities for further reading. (Indeed, for those entering the nationalist movement in the 1920s, prison was in a sense the nearest they came to going to a university.) Gandhi was clearly widely read; 'Certainly no other influential Indian intellectual was as steeped as Gandhi was', writes Raghavan Iyer, 'in the religious and philosophical texts of the classical Indian tradition as well as the writings of daring Western moralists of the nineteenth century like Tolstoy, Thoreau, Ruskin, Emerson and Carlyle' (1973, pp. 17–18). In some ways Gandhi was more the moralist than the intellectual; his was a quest for a moral philosophy, rather than delight in ideas for their own sake.

Karamchand Mohandas Gandhi was born on 2 October 1869, the fourth son of Hindu parents. Karamchand Gandhi and his wife, Putlibai, had married in 1857, when he was 47 years old and she 25 (strangely old by Indian standards). Gandhi was a child of his father's old age and especially cherished. He was born in the family home in Porbandar, a town of fishermen and sea-traders renowned for their shrewdness and toughness, but which was by then a sleepy little port on the decline.

At the time of Gandhi's birth his father was Dewan (prime minister) to the Thakor Saheb, princely ruler of Porbandar, which was one of the many small states in the Kathiawad peninsula. (Kathiawad has been renamed Saurasthra since independence.) This had become for the Gandhis almost, but not quite, a hereditary position. The family had settled in Porbandar in the mid-eighteenth century, purchasing the family home in 1777. Gandhi's grandfather, Uttamchand Gandhi, Dewan from 1813 to 1831, had been the most forceful of the family's servants of the state, his administration encouraging the East India Company to accord Porbandar status as a first-class state. Gandhi, as the brightest son, was thus the legatee of family expectation that he would take on an executive role as Dewan. His father, at the invitation of the Raj, moved to Rajkot in the 1870s, to take up the post of assessor of the Rajasthanik Court, a special court set up to sort out differences between the chiefs and vassals in Kathiawad feudal society. This was to bring the young Gandhi far more within the orbit of British rule, for Rajkot was the headquarters of the Resident, the representative of the Raj in the peninsula. It has been thought that Gandhi's birth in princely India greatly screened him from exposure to British rule – but this view should perhaps be modified. His father subsequently became Dewan to both the princely rulers of Rajkot and Wankaner. He died in 1886.

Gandhi is a natural prey for the psychobiographer. The extraordinarily intimate quality of his writings – his *Autobiography* (1927) being but the most obvious example of the continually open and frank way in which he discussed his inward and domestic life – reveals much fascinating detail of his psychological development. For the historian, however, there is always a danger that such an approach will lead attention too far away from the importance of Gandhi as a historical figure. That said, some attention has to be paid to the psychological approach as it brings us closer to an understanding of Gandhi's quest for identity.

Essentially Freudian insights into the psychological importance of family relationships have inherent limitations when applied to Indian family life, for they were drawn from a study of the late nineteenth-century bourgeois nuclear family, whereas India has an extended family system. Gandhi at Porbandar was certainly raised in an extended family as his father was head of a household shared by five brothers. Within the Indian extended family mother–son relationships tend to be especially intimate, almost stultifyingly so. The birth of a son raised the status of the mother within her new family and provided her with an emotional outlet in a traditional society where intimate ties between husband and wife were frowned on and only really grew in the later years of marriage. There is therefore nothing very exceptional in Gandhi's closeness to his mother. Indian women are customarily the transmitters of the traditional Hindu religious culture and Putlibai's most important legacy to her son was her own particular religious beliefs. She belonged to a sect especially opposed to idolatry, one which sought some bridge between Hinduism and Islam, and she had sympathy for Jainism, especially its emphases on the importance of vows (e.g. not to eat meat).

Psychologists both Western (e.g. Erikson) and Indian (e.g.

Sudhir Kakar) emphasize the strongly feminine character of Hindu culture, and it must be a matter of speculation whether Gandhi's identification with the feminine was a consequence of a specific relationships with his mother or the more pervasive influence of Hinduism. N. K. Bose has argued that 'Gandhi's desire to purify and civilize mankind lay within the depths of his personal relationship with his mother or to certain events of his boyhood days' (1953, p. 78). Gandhi identified with women, he postulated, because woman, with her capacity to endure suffering (especially in childbirth), seemed to him the incorporation of the ideal of non-violence or ahimsa. Erikson's account of the dominance of the 'maternal' in Gandhi's make-up, with his quest for service to the poor and untouchable, may likewise be open to criticism, but his suggestion that this' was Gandhi's pathway to Indian society, 'with a primitive mother religion' as 'probably the deepest, the most pervasive and the most unifying stratum of indian religiosity' (1970, p. 402) is more convincing.

Gandhi's relationship with his father, certainly in the short term, seems the more dynamic, though Western readers must not automatically assume this was purely Oedipal rivalry (in brief, Freud's theory of the Oedipus complex is that sons, even as infants, are sexually attracted to their mothers and thus jealous of their fathers), nor indeed that there was any sibling rivalry with his elder brothers. Gandhi had during his childhood to bear the burden of family hopes that he would succeed his father as Dewan or prime minister of a Kathiawad princely state. It seems more likely that Gandhi's rebelliousness as an adolescent lay less in any unconscious sexual rivalry for his mother than in the challenge of matching up to his father's expectations. Erikson has also stressed that the real crisis in growing up comes in adolescence when the son has to break from the father and acquire some personal system of belief or ideology in order to cope as an adult. In Indian society the father's presence tends to be less dominant and a father–son conflict less apparent, but filial deference is nevertheless deeply socialized. Gandhi's solution to the problem was unusual. On the journey from Rajkot to Porbandar to celebrate Gandhi's marriage in 1883 his father had a serious fall, and Gandhi took on the maternal role of nurse during his father's last years. Erikson claims this laid the foundation for the later strategy of non-violence: a style of leadership 'which can defeat a superior adversary only nonviolently and with the express intent of saving him as well as those whom he oppressed' (1970, p. 129). An event of exceptional significance in Gandhi's life was his neglecting his nursing duties towards his father to make love to his pregnant wife at the very time his father died. It was the traditional role of the eldest son to be present at his father's death and to light the funeral pyre, so it is symptomatic of Gandhi's seeing himself (despite being the youngest child) as the senior of his father's children that this betrayal was to cause him so much guilt. Maybe this feeling of betrayal, linked to so dynamic a source of guilt as sex, does much to explain Gandhi's acute moral conscience and feelings of guilt towards his father. But Erikson has argued that the real explanation lies at a deeper level; it derived from an awareness that through his own ability he would outshine and surpass his father.

It is well worth interjecting at this point the cautionary criticism that the tendency of the psychobiographer to stress the importance of early trauma may work rather poorly for Gandhi and that an alternative approach which emphasizes the continuing ability of the personality to respond to challenge throughout life may be far more convincing in his case (see W. M. Runyan, 1984, chapter 10).

Whereas the relations between Gandhi and his parents seem for the most part to be warm and supportive, those between him and his wife and children were often strained and in many ways form one of the most painful aspects of Gandhi's story. Maybe it is unfair to judge public figures by their private lives, but in the case of Gandhi, who recognized no such division between the public and the private, his family life has to be adjudged a reflection on his career. Gandhi's was a child marriage; he and Kasturbai, daughter of a Porbandar merchant, were both 13 at the time of their marriage. Kasturbai was illiterate and although Gandhi's attempts to educate her meant that in time she was able to read and write the Gujarati script with difficulty, theirs was never a marriage of minds. Moreover Kasturbai, far from showing deference to her husband, was wilful and there were famous moments of rebellion: for example, her refusal to empty 'cheerfully' as Gandhi insisted, the chamber pot of an 'untouchable' Christian staying at Phoenix Farm (the first of Gandhi's experimental centres for social reform) outside Durban. In time, however, she was to complement Gandhi's role as 'Bapu' or Father by being herself 'Ba' or Mother in Gandhi's ashrams (the name given to similar centres in India). Kasturbai, to quote one of Gandhi's biographers, was 'small, hardworking and level headed' (Ashe, 1968, p. 239). She shared Gandhi's imprisonments and died during his final internment at Poona, on 22 February 1944. If there was equanimity between them, it had been bought at a high price.

In 1906 Gandhi adopted a vow of brahmacharya or sexual abstinence. There were many contributory factors: an underlying sense of sexual guilt; anger at his father for subjecting him to sexual experience at so young an age; and at some level Gandhi no doubt shared a Hindu belief that all sex was weakening, a fatal diminution of vital fluid, which might otherwise be directed towards spiritual activity. Perhaps he felt there was some incompatibility between sexuality and his higher spiritual quest, and significantly the time of adoption of brahmacharya coincided with the beginning of satyagraha, Gandhi's technique of passive resistance. Kasturbai thus found herself a part of Gandhi's experiments with truth. (This did not stop him from exposing her to jealousy through the close emotional ties he was to establish with several other women.) Many defendants of Gandhi see in his marriage one of the most morally exemplary aspects of his life, perhaps particularly for Kasturbai's loyalty to him throughout the ashram years in India. Yet it is difficult for a Western reader not to feel some alienation from him because of his rejection of the values of physical love and his polarization of 'body-force' and 'soul-force'.

Gandhi's relations with his four sons were also flawed. Gandhi seemingly played the role of Victorian paterfamilias, but his sons all suffered from his refusal to allow them any formal education and his failure to find time to put his own theories of private education to the test. He put difficulties in the way of their marriages. Manilal (b. 1892) had to wait until he was 35; Ramdas (b. 1897) until he was 30; Devadas (b. 1900) sought a love match with the daughter of C. Rajagopalachari, Gandhi's outstanding advocate and ally in South India, an inter-caste marriage, which Gandhi insisted on delaying, although he was eventually to give his consent. It was Harilal, the eldest (b. 1888) who rebelled against his father, using the occasion of his marriage in 1911 to break away and go to live in Calcutta. Gandhi's refusal to support Harilal's second marriage in 1918 led to his increasing drunkenness and debt: when he converted to Islam in 1938 Gandhi ascribed it to mercenary reasons. He died shortly before his father's assassination. Ramdas (b. 1897) remained with Gandhi in the first of his Indian ashrams; the two other sons took up journalism – Manilal (b. 1892) as editor of *Indian Opinion* in South Africa, Devadas with the *Hindustan Times*. The family eventually settled down but, to quote Ashe again, 'it was sober-spirited, a little sad' (p. 95). Gandhi had taken his duties as 'householder' (the second stage in the Hindu life-cycle) in all seriousness, but it was an 'experiment' of limited success.

This account of family life still leaves uncharted any description of the fashioning of Gandhi's ideology – his social and political philosophy. One might begin with his education. In Rajkot he first attended the primary school, then went on to Alfred High School. This was an English medium school (where all lessons were in English) with some of the trappings of the English public school, for example playing cricket, and his attendance there marks the beginning of Gandhi's acculturation as a 'brown Briton'. Although Gandhi went to the college at Bhavnagar for a year, the family decided that only an education in England would guarantee his future role as Dewan and restore the faltering fortunes of the family in an increasingly anglicized Kathiawad. It led to the momentous decision to 'cross the black waters' in September 1888, which meant ostracism by his modh bania caste community (never to be withdrawn by the branches in Porbandar and Bombay, though Gandhi was to make his peace with his caste community in Rajkot on his return). He enrolled at the Inner Temple, where his 'higher' education culminated with examinations in Roman and Common Law. He qualified in June 1890. He had also found time to take the University of London matriculation, with Latin, French, English Language, History, Geography and Science, among his subjects. No teacher seems to have left at any stage any special impression on the young Gandhi: intellectual stimulus came from elsewhere. None the less, his legal training and practice gave Gandhi a 'British' identity he was not to cast off until some 15 years later, long into his stay in South Africa.

The London years were crucial for his intellectual growth, for it was then, through his joining the London Vegetarian Society, that he was introduced to the ideas of two writers who were greatly to influence his own work – Tolstoy (1828–1910), Russian aristocrat, novelist and moralist, and Ruskin (1819–1900), one of the great Victorian moralists, a social thinker, an art historian and critic. But it was his encounter with Madame Blavatsky and Annie Besant of the Theosophical Society which was perhaps even more significant. Through them he came to learn how highly some Europeans regarded Hindu religion and philosophy. (The Theosophical Society had been founded in America in 1875 by a Colonel Olcott but moved its headquarters to India in 1882. The quest of the society was spiritual and their growing aim was to discover a new 'world teacher'. It was Madame Blavatsky who especially emphasized the importance of Indian religions; Annie Besant, ex-atheist and champion of birth-control, took over the running of the Theosophical Society in Madras and was later to become a leading figure in the Indian National Congress. Gandhi himself only ever became an associate member of the society, and this was for but a six-month period in 1896 while he was in Durban.) It was in his attempted role as Sanskrit translator for some Theosophical Society friends that Gandhi first discovered the *Bhagavad-Gita* – albeit in Edwin Arnold's English translation *The Song Celestial*. (The *Gita*, part of the Indian religious classic, the Mahabharata, is one of the most sacred texts of Hinduism.) Paradoxically, it was this 'discovery' of his own culture that constituted Gandhi's greatest debt to the West.

Gandhi read Tolstoy's *The Kingdom of God is Within You* in Durban, quite shortly after its publication and translation into English in 1894. It was clearly a seminal text in Gandhi's conversion to non-violence; in his view a far more convincing apologia than that by any Indian author. Gandhi was familiar with other moralistic writings of Tolstoy but this was the work that 'overwhelmed' him and 'left an abiding impression' (Gandhi, 1927, p. 84). If the personal circumstances of the Russian aristocrat and the aspiring Indian lawyer were worlds apart, those of Russia and India in the 1890s were not, and it is not in the least surprising that a moral conscience outraged by tsarist autocracy and Russian serfdom should have sounded an echo within Gandhi, a man soon to be embattled with the Raj and campaigning on behalf of the Indian peasantry.

Did Gandhi acquire his belief in non-violence from Tolstoy or did Tolstoy merely confirm in him a belief he already held? There was a seeming contradiction in Tolstoy's own defence of non-violence. On the one hand, he argued the case for non-violence on the ground that as no one can agree on the nature of evil, no one has a monopoly of the truth: perhaps this was

9

simply a plea for toleration. On the other hand, however, he presents a specifically Christian, and hence exclusive message, in his plea for the progressive absorption of Christian ethics, as only such spiritual enlightenment will pave the way for a new society. No doubt Tolstoy's attack on modern society and the state acted as a catalyst for Gandhi's anti-urbanism and may have fatally infected him with a distrust not only for a 'law and order' state but a welfare one as well. For all his moral anger, Tolstoy seems essentially to be making a rhetorical statement, and his arguments on non-violence were a good deal softer-edged than those of Gandhi.

Gandhi first read Ruskin's *Unto this Last* (published in 1862) in 1904, while on a train journey from Johannesburg to Durban. It was a book, he said, 'that brought about an instantaneous and practical transformation in my life. I believe that I discovered some of my deepest convictions reflected in the great book of Ruskin' (1927, p. 182). Did he really understand it? It is a complex, almost impenetrable, book. Together with Carlyle, Ruskin was the greatest of the Victorian moralists, and Gandhi may above all have been responding to that quality of high moral conscience on social questions. Ruskin was a High Tory, and his book was a critique of the *laissez-faire* utilitarian values of nineteenth-century liberalism, although it did not, by any means, preach structural change and egalitarianism. Its signal importance for Gandhi perhaps lay in its high evaluation of work, especially that of the artisan: the notion of the redemptive quality of labour was something Gandhi could not have learned from his own tradition, indeed could only have learned from the West. Ruskin's writings may have reinforced in Gandhi's mind his conservative concept of trusteeship – the belief literally that all property is held in trust to God, though Gandhi came to see this more in terms of property-owners exercising a proper sense of social responsibility – but they may also have acted as a mental trigger for his growing disillusionment with, and hostility to, capitalism. Significantly he translated the book into Gujarati under the title *Sarvodaya*, meaning the welfare of all, the key concept of his economic and social programme.

Another work that impressed Gandhi was Edward Carpenter's *Civilisation: Its Cause and Cure*, published in London in 1891. (Gandhi referred to Carpenter in *Hind Swaraj* as 'a great English writer'.) There are revealing similarities between late Victorian/ Edwardian moralists such as Carpenter and Gandhi in their increasing alienation from Victorian civilization and their quest for new values. They agreed that there was a profound need to harmonize the private and public needs of the individual. But the divergences are equally striking. Whereas Carpenter, as a homosexual, sought to throw off the hypocrisies and constraints of Victorian views on sexuality, Gandhi rejected the physical claims of love. Carpenter, while rejecting the materialist culture of capitalism, saw that salvation lay in passing through industrialism to some post-industrial socialist society; Gandhi turned Luddite and looked backwards. One vision was utopian, the other arcadian. But if a European moralist like Carpenter experienced alienation through the way 'civilization' had cut man off from nature and community, such alienation posed a much more devastating threat to a Hindu, for whom it was conterminous with ostracism and outcasting, the sovereign sanction of caste—Hindu society against its offenders.

In 1909 in the Gujarati journal *Indian Opinion*, which he edited in South Africa, Gandhi published *Hind Swaraj* (Indian Home Rule), a text generally interpreted as signalling his rejection of Western civilization. It may be, however, that such a view overestimates the extent to which he had assimilated Western values. The text has far greater significance as an affirmation of Gandhi's faith in Indian culture. He branded Western civilization as godless; that of India, in contrast, was one that 'elevated the moral being', one that believed in God. Gandhi's greater concern may have been not so much to denigrate western values as to berate those Indians, especially the professional men, doctors and lawyers, who had betrayed Indian values and had become 'Westernized'. If such was Gandhi's negative judgement on the West, how had he come to discover the positive values of Indian civilization?

Gandhi was a Hindu by birth and upbringing, and obviously this had far more influence in shaping his absorption of Hindu values than his study of Western writers. His family belonged to a Bhaktic sect, the Vallabhacharya Sampradeya, that is one devoted to the worship of Krishna and Sri Rama (avatars or reincarnations of the preserver god Vishnu). He thus belonged to the Vaishnavite branch of Hinduism rather than the Shaivite (i.e. worshippers of the destroyer god Siva). His earliest memories of Hinduism were of the Ramayana, the great Indian religious classic on the struggle between Rama and Ravana, and the cult of Ram was deeply to influence his religious beliefs. 'Ram' took

11

the place of 'God' in his daily prayers. Kathiawad was the home of Jainism, and Gandhi deeply absorbed its ideals, above all that of ahimsa or non-violence, both through his mother and Raychambai (a diamond merchant, philosopher and poet, who was aged 25 at the time Gandhi met him on his return from England in 1891).

Such experiences rendered possible Gandhi's communication with the Indian masses: it created a means of linking a folk culture with the higher Sanskritic culture he was to absorb. As Erikson concludes, Gandhi came in time to recognize that this ancient religious culture was the one factor holding an intensely pluralist Indian society together and constituted the absolutely indispensable medium for communication with the Indian masses (1970, pp. 396–9). But Gandhi was in no way a typical Hindu, and in many respects his ideas were heretical in origin. He did not worship in temples. Prayer meetings in the ashrams owed more to Christian practice. Although he strongly disliked Christian evangelicals with their claim to a unique revealed truth, there was a link between the evangelical insistence on conscience and divine guidance and Gandhi's reliance on his inner voice, that 'daimon' of Socrates which so fascinated him (he was to make a Gujarati translation of Plato's *Trial of Socrates*). Jainism was the religion of the merchant or bania communities of Kathiawad, who were in opposition to control by the higher brahmin caste over social and religious observances. Kathiawad had earlier given birth to another dynamic social reformer, Dayanand Saraswati, whose Arya Samaj movement, if in part inspired by a wish to restore brahmin dominance, was itself highly unorthodox. The role of sanyasin, or itinerant saint, assumed by Gandhi, was one recognized way of escaping brahminical constraints.

Two ideals lay at the centre of Gandhi's philosophy, satya, 'truth', and ahimsa, 'non-violence'. The uniqueness of his approach, to use Raghavan Iyer's argument, was to stress their interdependence. We generally translate satya as truth and there is a temptation to see it as a metaphysical correlate to Western concepts, to a mystical view of the Absolute. Although this may be valid, the word does contain other meanings – real, sincere, existent, pure, good, effectual (Iyer, 1973, p. 145); or put another way, 'truthfulness, an openness and concentration on the essential points of every issue' (Rothermund, 1963, p. 65). Gandhi saw the essence of dharma, the underlying social morality of Hinduism, as satya, and this was crucial for the dissemination of his ideas, for dharma was a far more familiar concept to Indians. Dharma means good conduct: it underlies the caste system and is clearly a highly conservative philosophy.

The link between satya and ahimsa is hard to grasp. Ahimsa literally means 'non-injury'. Gandhi extended its range of meaning to include, on the negative side, hurt by lying or evil thoughts; on the positive side, the need for pity, suffering, love. The link between satya and ahimsa can be highly metaphysical – to quote Margaret Chatterjee: 'since our views of the truth are but fragmentary, no man must impose his partial vision on others: this is the foundation for Gandhi's belief in non-violence' (1983, p. 74). Such uncertainties led Gandhi to characterize his various moral quests as 'experiments with truth' and perhaps in this way he avoided the inconsistency in Tolstoy's philosophy. Gandhi's claim that ahimsa lay at the heart of satya was interesting and by itself unorthodox: the ancient Vedic texts, the sacred writings of early Hinduism, make no such claims for ahimsa, and the concept only percolated into Hinduism through the rival faiths of Jainism and Buddhism. Gandhi was effectively arguing in a highly innovative and heretical way.

If Gandhi's religious beliefs were not founded on the traditional texts, there was one work that profoundly influenced his practice, the *Bhagavad-Gita*. Here again, however, his interpretation was highly original. The *Gita* is a central text in the Vedantic culture of modern India. It seems clear that it is a conservative defence of dharma: the warrior, Arjuna, on being confronted by the moral dilemma of whether to fight his relatives, seeks the advice of the god Krishna; he is told that his higher loyalty is to his caste dharma or duty as a kshatriya or warrior and that he must fight. Admittedly he is admonished that he must do so with no pursuit of personal gain, in a spirit of non-attachment. Krishna instructs Arjuna: 'Prepare for war with peace in thy soul. Be in peace in pleasure and pain, in gain and in loss, in victory or in the loss of a battle. In this peace there is no sin' (Mascaro, 1953, p. 51). Possibly such language permitted Gandhi his own idiosyncratic interpretation. Krishna, he believed, was in fact advocating non-violent action. The poem should be seen, according to Gandhi, as a commentary not on a real battle but on an internal one within the soul. Krishna sees Arjuna as 'merely the means of my work' and this may be the clue to Gandhi's extracting from the text his belief in the dynamics of means shaping ends.

If the prevailing orthodoxy in modern Hinduism is Vedantic, based on the Vedas and essentially other-worldly in outlook, the thrust of Gandhi's philosophy was quite otherwise. He belonged to a relatively neglected part of the Hindu tradition, to the Kharma-Yogi, a tradition of action, of an essentially 'this-world-ly' approach. Admittedly he drew on a similar tradition of ascetic practices or tapas (tapascharya were the meditations and austerities of the saints); devotion to satya and ahimsa are paramount examples, brahmacharya another. Gandhi had a Hindu view of time, seeing the world as caught up in a vast cyclical process, with the present age, the Black or Kali Yuga age, some five thousand years old. He thus did not share a nineteenth-century Western faith in a linear view of progress. His vision was arcadian, a looking back to an age of truth, to Satya Yuga, when the Kingdom of God, or Ram Rajha, had been realized on earth. Yet he shared the views of an earlier utopian socialist, Charles Fourier, that immediate steps could be taken to realize utopia. Fourier had written of moving from an age of 'civilization' to an age of 'harmony', in his cyclical scheme, from the fifth age to the eighth. Whereas Fourier had put his faith in his 'phalansteries', his utopian (quasi-socialist) communities, Gandhi's was in the ashrams, his centres for social reform and spiritual training. Such a realization of the Kingdom of God upon earth was very different from the ideal of a liberation from the world expressed in the Vedas.

Gandhi's was to be a lifetime of testing out means, of experiments. One such experiment had been his vegetarianism in London, the beginnings of a lifelong experiment with diet. (Even if Gandhi rejected sex, he always paid attention to the physical needs of the body.) The most formative years of Gandhian experimentation in means, or different sorts of action, were to be in South Africa, 'that God-forsaken continent where I found my God' (Chatterjee, 1983, p. 48). To that stage of his life we must now turn.

2 South Africa: Satyagraha or passive resistance

In South Africa Gandhi confronted a society as stratified and pluralist as his own in India. One needs to stress the length of time he spent there – 21 years – and that, as he arrived there at the age of 22, these were his formative adult years. They were years of a profound evolution in mind and commitment; lessons were learned of exceptional consequence for his future struggle in India. The degree to which he grasped the character of power and race in South Africa, however, remains contentious. These adult years have also to be assessed in terms of Gandhi's contribution to the solution of political and social tensions during the emergent years of apartheid.

The journey to South Africa was for Gandhi a means of escape from increasingly unmanageable demands in Kathiawad. On his return to India in 1891 he learned of his mother's death during his absence in England. The expectations of his family were yet to be fulfilled; Gandhi had turned aside from local political ambition, but he had also failed to make any headway in his chosen career as a lawyer. An attempt to advance his brother Laxmidas's career by approaching the British agent at Porbandar, whom he had briefly met in London, likewise turned to embarrassment: he was accused of abusing friendship and forcibly evicted from the house. In retrospect Gandhi absorbed a far-reaching lesson from this set-back in that he subsequently placed a public ethic of incorruptibility above all sectional demands of family, caste or community, a value system with devastating implications for Indian society.

There was nothing extraordinary in a firm of Muslim merchants in Durban approaching Gandhi to come out to South Africa to settle a legal dispute. Muslim merchants from Porbandar in particular may have sought out trading opportunities elsewhere with the decline of their home port, but Gujarati merchants had for centuries traded with East Africa, and South Africa was a natural extension of their commercial enterprise. Moreover Gandhi was quite a catch as a London-trained lawyer. He arrived in Durban during May 1893.

There was no reason why Gandhi should have acquired any awareness of the full ramifications of the social and political circumstances in which he was now to find himself. Indeed, Gandhi's instinct was to concentrate on the specific and he may never have plumbed the general character of the situation in South Africa during the following two decades. For the student of Gandhi it is important to have some grasp of the nature of that development, for more than any other experience to date it was to shape his response to modern capitalism and industrialization.

He had already witnessed the impact of modernization on his society in the Kathiawad province: railways putting the boatmen out of business, new cotton-spinning factories displacing the traditional craftsmen. He may have drawn conclusions from his experience of such large cities as London and Bombay. But nothing could have brought home to him so vividly the character of modern capitalism than the Klondike atmosphere of Johannesburg. In 1886 the Witwatersrand reef was responsible for 0.16 per cent of the world output of gold; in 1898, 27.7 per cent, by 1913, 40 per cent.

In terms of the impact of these developments on the governing elite of this new society, for a long time the received view was of a society of farmers ('Boer' means farmer) increasingly drawn into this mining revolution, threatened by foreigners ('uitlanders'), and above all by British capitalists, a new elite, typified by Cecil Rhodes. The recent scholarship of Charles Van Onselen, however, has considerably modified this account. We can now see the Boers, led by Kruger in the then independent South African Republic, as also committed to capitalist expansion but with alternative priorities and at a more gradual pace. The Boer War of 1899–1902 was 'not so much a dispute over the desirability of capitalism as a goal for the Transvaal as a conflict between two competing bourgeoisies about the terms and paths along which it could best be sought' (Van Onselen, 1982, I, p. 23). Kruger was anxious to further the interests of Boer capitalist farmers, who could make a profit from the opportunities of selling food surpluses and above all from the liquor trade serving these new urban communities. According to Van

16

Onselen, his vision of a 'republic founded on an agricultural base with an industrial growth' was, however, to be eclipsed by 'the mining revolution' (I, p. 38). For Gandhi, increasingly alienated from modern capitalism, there was not, after all, so much to choose between British and Boer values.

Such phenomena, however, were certainly not at the heart of Gandhi's rejection of this modern Babylon. Van Onselen writes also of 'a fundamentally warped social fabric' (I, p. 104) in Johannesburg: a gross imbalance in the ratio of the sexes, a lack of stable family life with a male-dominated society of whites and blacks alike. The flourishing sale of alcohol was one way of controlling the unstable labour force; organized vice was another. In 1896, for example, ten per cent of all white women over 15 years of age were prostitutes. Indian landlords in Durban were but one of many groups who had profited from organized vice. In time both Boer and Briton sought to check the consumption of alcohol and the spread of prostitution, none more vigorously than Smuts, the young Attorney-General of the South African Republic, in 1899. But prostitution remained a feature of this new society and one that must have concerned Gandhi deeply. Gandhi's story is linked to this social malaise in a way that has been previously overlooked. The new Boer government of the Transvaal of 1907 sought to deport the pimps and prostitutes under the very same law, the Immigrants Restriction Act, the Black Act, of 1907, through which it tried to limit the number of Indians in the Transvaal.

The Indians came to form a sizeable minority in South Africa through the pressing economic need of this burgeoning capitalism for cheap labour. The demand here came not from the Randlords (the new capitalists in the gold mines) but from the sugar planters of Natal. This story has to be briefly sketched if Gandhi's career in South Africa is to be understood.

Natal itself had become a Crown Colony in 1856. Between 1860 and 1911, 152,184 indentured Indian labourers came to work on the sugar plantations of Natal. Initially they were indentured for five years, but in time this was limited to two, and they were expected either to serve their indentures or to return to India. Other Natal capitalists began to see advantages in this form of labour recruitment, and Indians found themselves indentured also in the coalfields and in other capitalist concerns. Such reliance on a force of quasi slave labour is an index of how diseased a form of capitalism was evolving in South Africa.

The abolition of this labour system raises an interpretative controversy analogous to that over the negro slave system that preceded it. Was it phased out after 1911 because of economic factors or for humanitarian reasons? There can be no doubt that the government of India took an increasing interest in the plight of indentured labourers when it became apparent that the impoverished low caste and tribal people who were being syphoned off as a welcome relief from the pressure of India's surplus population might in fact be as profitably employed in the new cash crop economy of India, in those expanding agro-industries of tea, coffee and sisal. There seems to be some uncertainty among historians as to the character of Gandhi's relationship with the indentured Indian community. Clearly he could not be unaware of them, but whether one should argue that he only reluctantly reached out to expose their grievances, for they did not become involved in any large number in the passive resistance (satyagraha) campaign until 1913 (see below), or that Gandhi's was a persistent but uphill struggle to break down their inertia and indifference, remains in dispute.

Self-evidently, even if indentured labour provided an economic opportunity for impoverished Indians, there was something profoundly humiliating to an Indian in the nature of such employment. But this does not necessarily get to the heart of the sense of outrage within Indian public opinion at the indentured labour system. This was, in fact, another example of Van Onselen's 'fundamentally warped social fabric', with its evils of an imbalance of the sexes and lack of family life. Indian 'womanhood' was subject to abuse; prostitution and venereal disease were on the increase. Charles Andrews, an English missionary and opponent of the system, later to be a devoted follower of Gandhi, had first discovered such matters among indentured Indians in Fiji, but the situation also prevailed in Natal. This became, in India, the basis of a profound moral imperative for change, and it was one that Gandhi shared.

If Gandhi was drawn into this issue, however, there is very little evidence that he responded with equal concern to the plight of African labour. This is not the place to describe the condition of Africans in the compounds of the new mining industries, but African farming communities were put under great pressure and it now became quite deliberate government policy to break up African agriculture to force Africans into the labour market of the mines. The lesson that Gandhi was to draw from exposure

18

to such social squalor was the need to reinforce village agriculture and to protect the Indian peasantry from such a vile alternative.

The indentured Indian labourers, who constituted the majority of Indians in South Africa, were their most deprived and under-privileged stratum. The elite among the Indians, styled 'passengers' as they had paid for their boat passage, were largely members of the Muslim merchant community – Gandhi's presence, both as a fully trained professional lawyer and, if to a lesser degree, as a well-off Hindu, was exceptional. However, the community of 'free' Indians was expanding all the time: Indians who had worked their indentures either stayed on in South Africa or many, after a brief visit to India, returned. These poorer Indians turned to petty trade, often as hawkers, or to market gardening. In all, the 'free Indians' became an increasingly influential commercial community, serving the needs of some whites and virtually monopolizing those of the blacks. The vast proportion of Indians, more than 80 per cent, was concentrated in Natal, where they formed a significant minority. In 1896 Natal's population comprised 400,000 blacks, 50,000 whites and 51,000 Indians. It was a measure of the efficacy of migration control that the proportion of Indians in the population elsewhere was considerably smaller. The Orange Free State successfully closed its frontier to Indians, but by 1904 there were 10,192 in Cape Province. According to the 1904 census for the Transvaal there were 11,321 Indians (mainly merchants), 299,000 whites and 945,000 Africans (Hunt, 1978, p. 46). These numbers were enough to cause white racist fears of an 'Asian peril'. This racism came as much from English migrants to South Africa, a white-collar and petty bourgeois class who felt threatened in their occupations (mainly clerical) and commercial interests by the Indian presence, as from the substantial Afrikaaner population. The latter, drawn off the farms by the agrarian changes of the late nineteenth century and increasingly marginalized in the cities, had been driven into such declining activities as cab-driving or brick-making. It was, then, in the defence of this 'free Indian' community against racial discrimination that, to a large extent, the young Gandhi became embattled on his arrival in South Africa.

Gandhi came to a country where the struggle for political power lay between the competing white elites of Britons and Boers. He shared some of the liberal perception of the Boers as being themselves victims of colonial oppression, although he was

19

curiously reluctant to act on this awareness. He came to South Africa still believing in the imperial rhetoric of Queen Victoria's Proclamation of 1 November 1858, with its promise of equality before the law for all citizens of the British Empire. Gandhi's faith in the liberal promise of empire clung to him throughout the South African years and explains, no doubt, his readiness to support the British, with his raising of an Indian brigade during the Boer War and again during the savage suppression of Zulu resistance during the 1906 Bambata rising in Natal. In South Africa there was some justification for his approval of the empire, for the British colonial presence had certainly introduced liberal principles into the Constitution of Cape Colony, both with the franchise for the Cape coloured peoples and the independent judiciary, and through the attempts of evangelical missionaries to mitigate the work conditions of blacks. Natal, however, was a newer colony and its administrative structures were far more paternalist. To a large degree Gandhi struggled for liberal concessions for Natal on a par with those prevailing in Cape Colony. Joseph Chamberlain, Colonial Secretary since 1895, and Sir Alfred Milner, High Commissioner in South Africa since 1897, were also largely to revive such liberal rhetoric, in terms of Britain protecting the interests not only of the Indians but also of the blacks, by way of fashioning a moral *raison d'être* for declaring war in 1899.

Gandhi also came up against colonialism following his move to Johannesburg in 1902, in the shape of Milner's post-war administration. The Transvaal itself was, in the aftermath of war, a special case, but in general no legislation could be passed in a colonial legislature without parliamentary and royal assent in London, so inevitably the focus of power was still seen to be metropolitan, and this explains Gandhi's visits to London to plead the Indians' case in 1907 and in 1909. It was not until 1907 that he was forced to deal directly with an Afrikaaner-controlled government in the Transvaal, and this brought him into conflict with a far more ideologically engrained racism. These constraints determined the type of politics Gandhi was to pursue at the outset, essentially those of petition and bargaining. Some time was to elapse before the entirely different strategy of non-violent resistance emerged.

Early after his arrival in South Africa in 1893 Gandhi underwent a humiliation that profoundly shaped his attitude to living there. (He had already had one minor brush with the authorities, but here had compromised: he had agreed to take off his turban in the court in Durban while sorting out his client's affairs.) On his journey to Pretoria, by train from Durban to Charlestown, a white passenger objected to Gandhi's presence in a first-class carriage and he was forcibly removed from the train and, together with his luggage, dumped on the platform at Pietermaritzburg, exposing him both to insult and to an exceptionally cold night. Almost immediately Gandhi had experienced what it was like to be designated a 'coolie', that term of insult for Indians in South Africa. (In fact, 'coolie' refers both to a name for an Indian hill tribe and to an urban labourer.) It was then that Gandhi decided he would have to stay on in South Africa, to 'root out the disease of colour prejudice', and to 'suffer hardship in the process' (Gandhi, 1927, p. 68). The following evening he continued, first class, on his rail journey to Charlestown. There was an almost similar embarrassment on the next stage, a coach journey, when it looked as if Gandhi would be refused a seat in the carriage and would have to sit on the footboard as a 'sami' (another term of racial abuse for Indians). On this occasion his fellow passengers came to his rescue. When he was subsequently refused a first-class rail ticket between Johannesburg and Pretoria, Gandhi, using his legal knowledge, checked the rail regulations to find that no such regulation applied to Indians, and thus completed his journey first class. It is a measure of the distance that Gandhi was, metaphorically, to travel that later he would *choose* to travel third class. At this stage his viewpoint was still one of Indian assimilation to the establishment, but there were now significant changes in his approach. Once a diffident public speaker, on his arrival he called a meeting of Indians in Pretoria (not in fact a large population) in order to form an Indian community, which could then more effectively protest about its grievances. His assimilationist tactics were evident, however, in his encouraging his audience to learn English as a means of self-advancement.

Gandhi then returned to Durban and started to build up a very lucrative practice as a lawyer. He earned his fees mainly by finding loopholes in the law for his merchant clients, both rich and poor, subject as they were to a variety of constraints in their commercial practices.

His first major encounter with the colonial government came a year after his arrival, when, in April 1894, he discovered the intent of the Natal authorities to deprive Indians of the right to vote. Gandhi's complaint lay in the disenfranchising of the Indians on grounds of race (he was perfectly happy for non-racial limitations to be introduced, for example disqualification on grounds of insufficient property). He would have settled for a similar franchise to that of the coloureds in Cape Colony, which applied to those possessing property worth £75 or an annual income of £50. Gandhi lost in the Natal legislature but the bill was blocked at Westminster. It was in response to this challenge that on 22 May 1894 Gandhi launched a political association, the Natal Indian Congress, to fight for the rights of the Natal Indians. One of its first achievements was to pressure the government into reducing a prospective £25 a year poll tax on all Indians to £3, though this itself later became one of the major grievances of the Indian community.

On his return to Durban at the end of December 1896, after a brief visit to India, Gandhi discovered the extent to which he had become the focus of racist hostility among Durban whites and their racist fears of uncontrolled Indian immigration. A crowd of some 3,300 had gathered to oppose the landing of 600 Indians. The wife of the superintendent of police in Durban, Mrs Alexander, rescued Gandhi from the crowd and later he was smuggled to safety out of the police station dressed as a policeman. (It is worth consulting Pyarelal (1980, vol II, pt I) for a marvellous set-piece account of the incident.) In 1897 the Indian community found itself subject to a series of restrictive measures and it was but slight recompense for Gandhi that he came in time to win the respect of Harry Escombe, the former Attorney-General, and, in 1897, Prime Minister of Natal.

It is important to stress that at this stage Gandhi fought for Indians as a distinctive community. There was no inherent sympathy between the Indians and the coloured community, and the gulf, as Gandhi saw it, between Indian and 'Kaffir' was too great to bridge. Indeed, Gandhi saw as quite legitimate the fears of the white community that they might be overwhelmed by the African majority. Indians came, he claimed, from a higher culture and rightly sought equality with the British; they were to be differentiated from the 'Kaffirs'.

The liberal rhetoric that accompanied the British involvement in the Boer War may have misled Gandhi into supposing that the Indian minority was now in new, safe hands. In 1901 he left South Africa for India, seemingly for good. In fact, little had been resolved. Lord Milner's post-war period of reconstruction sought above all to set up an industrial base for the further expansion of capitalism: it was essential that a labour policy should be designed to complement that ambition. This inevitably meant that most of the pre-war promises about labour policy proved empty; the grievances of the Indian community, if somewhat marginal, were likewise to be neglected. Milner set up a registrar of Asiatics. A thumb-print registration would permit the Indians right of residence. But all the constraints of the earlier (1885) Boer legislation in the Transvaal were reimposed. Indians were denied the right to own real estate and to vote; they were confined to specific locations, had to pay a £3 poll tax and were required to register. Antagonism to Indian immigration into the Transvaal ran high: even those Indians who had left because of the war found it difficult to re-enter. Gandhi returned with the aim of presenting the case of the Indians of both Natal and the Transvaal to Chamberlain, the British Colonial Secretary, who was on a flying visit to South Africa. He had in fact returned to embark on a far more critical struggle against racism.

Gandhi now moved to Johannesburg: here lay the real challenge. In 1903 he added the press to his armoury by starting up a weekly called *Indian Opinion*. In 1906, following his return from the Zulu war, where he had been a sergeant-major in charge of 24 Indian stretcher-bearers, Gandhi heard of Lionel Curtis's proposal for the Transvaal Asiatic Law Amendment Ordinance, to be published on 12 August 1906 and which required all Indians to register yet again (with prints of all ten fingers this time, not just one!), men and women alike. (Lionel Curtis was Assistant Colonial Secretary in the Transvaal and close to Lord Milner.) Anyone who failed to register would be subject to a fine, imprisonment or deportation. Admittedly, in mitigation, the £3 tax was to go. However, the colonial administration had clearly surrendered to the white community's fears of an influx of Asians. This measure was a deliberate attempt to harass Asians, to deter them from coming and induce them to leave. Although initiated by a colonial administration, it reflected an Afrikaaner hope that the Indian question would miraculously go away, simply by repatriation.

The prospect of this ordinance led to the famous meeting in the English Theatre in Johannesburg on 11 September 1906. The meeting was convened not by Gandhi but by an Indian merchant, Hajee Ojer Ally. It was the declaration at the meeting of another Muslim merchant, Hajee Habib, that in the name of God he would not submit to this legislation that inspired Gandhi to elevate his proposal to refuse to register to the level of a solemn vow of resistance. This proved to be the beginning of Gandhian passive resistance.

The days of colonial rule were running out in South Africa. At the Peace Treaty of Vereeniging which concluded the Boer War on 31 May 1902, General Jan Smuts had already been alerted to the likelihood that a new Liberal administration at Westminster would reverse the colonial status of the Transvaal and the Orange Free State in favour of self-government. In retrospect, the Milner administration in South Africa had pioneered neo-colonialism: it seemed as long as trading and financial profits were received, there was little to be lost in granting a subject colonial people self-rule. Astonishingly, Gandhi had still not lost faith in the empire and these years from 1906 mark a peculiarly divided period in his life. On the one hand he continued to act the role of the English lawyer, pleading the case of those he represented to the British establishment; on the other hand he was gradually taking on the role of rebel against colonial rule.

When Liberal Party leader Campbell-Bannerman came to power in 1905, and the Liberals achieved a landslide election victory in 1906, it looked as though Gandhi's case had an excellent chance of being heard in London. Surely the presence of that most liberal of political thinkers, Lord Morley, as Secretary of State for India, boded well for his success? Gandhi found he had to deal, however, with an unimaginative Secretary of State for the Colonies in Lord Elgin (a former Viceroy) but with a far more lively Under-Secretary in Winston Churchill (the beginnings of a long encounter between two exceptional personalities). Gandhi, obscuring his role as a radical, tried to exploit every contact he could within the English establishment. None the less he failed in his major objective, the setting up of a Commission of Inquiry, which would repudiate racist rumours of an 'Asian peril' and investigate Indian grievances. But he had seemingly achieved a victory in Elgin's agreement to postpone the implementation of Curtis's ordinance.

Gandhi returned to South Africa in December 1906 in some euphoria. He had, however, been fooled. The Liberal administration had simply delegated responsibility; it was left to the new administration in the self-governing Transvaal to introduce such measures after the elections to its own legislature in January

24

1907. The new government, led by General Botha, with Smuts as his Colonial Secretary, proceeded to do so in the Immigrants Restriction Act of 1907. This became law on 1 July – the notorious Black Act as it came to be called. (Gandhi now experienced his first period of imprisonment when sentenced to two months with hard labour on 10 January 1908 for refusing to register.) Gandhi returned to London again in 1909, placing his faith this time in a former Governor of Madras, Lord Ampthill, and seeking no more than concessions for educated Indians (whom the whites feared the most) to enter the Transvaal. Ampthill, if no friend of Indian nationalism, gave Gandhi his support, but Smuts would not yield on the racial terms of the Act. This second visit seems to have completed his disillusionment with empire, for he was now to turn his back on London, the rhetoric of empire and Western civilization. Indeed it was during his return journey in 1909 that he wrote *Hind Swaraj* (Indian Home Rule), the key document in Gandhi's discovery of himself as an Indian nationalist. The empire was now seen as offering slavery, not partnership; Gandhi's protest was as much against this wider failure as against specific grievances in the Transvaal.

During the Transvaal civil rights campaign between 1907 and 1913 Gandhi tested out and gave shape to the essential elements of his technique of passive, non-violent resistance – satyagraha. The protest concentrated on two complaints: the need to register under the Black Act and those further restrictions introduced by the Transvaal government on Indian right of entry to the Transvaal. But the wider issue of racism was also in dispute. Gandhi had no objection to registration or immigration controls as such; it was their imposition on grounds of race, that is, of being Indian, that inspired the campaign. One highly contentious principle of satyagraha emerged early on: the readiness to respond to an opponent's proposal of compromise. When Smuts offered to reconsider the Black Act on condition that Indians registered voluntarily, Gandhi agreed to meet him – the first of many encounters between Gandhi, on release from gaol, and those in authority. Gandhi trusted Smuts and satyagraha was lifted. The Indians registered, but the Black Act remained. Gandhi's reply to Smut's betrayal was the famous occasion on 16 August 1908 when, outside the Haminia Mosque in Johannesburg, thousands of the registration certificates, old as well as new, were burned.

25

The second phase of satyagraha was more determined. In October 1908 Gandhi was arrested again, this time for illegally crossing the state frontier. Organizing satyagraha took up most of Gandhi's time and his legal practice was virtually suspended. He could only rely on 100 active 'satyagrahis', that is men who would be ready to go on being arrested time and again. At one stage, however (by November 1909), Gandhi claimed that some 2,500 of the 13,000 Transvaal Indians had been arrested. He was particularly anxious that the educated Indians and the wealthy merchant class should set an example. He accused the former of preying on the needy, poorer Indians; the latter of often being ready to sit back, secure in the trading licences they had already obtained. He wrote: 'if out of selfishness and intoxication of wealth they sacrifice the interests of the community, they will feel sorry for themselves later. Putting up with small losses now will save them from big losses in future' (*Indian Opinion*, 2 April 1910). Gandhi showed considerable talent in such cajoling of moral sensibility. In May 1910 Tolstoy Farm was set up outside Johannesburg as a refuge for families whose lives had been disrupted by the campaign. The Black Act eventually became unenforceable, but there was no resolution to the conflict.

The climax came in the aftermath of Gokhale's visit (he was leader of the Indian National Congress) to South Africa in 1912. Once again Smuts made offers that were not to be fulfilled. He offered to withdraw the Black Act, and, technically, he did so at the Transvaal level but it was simply re-enacted as Union legislation. He offered to withdraw the £3 tax still imposed on ex-indentured labourers in Natal. But something quite different was to reactivate satyagraha – a Supreme Court decision that Hindu, Muslim and Parsee marriages were invalid. This effectively branded all Indian wives mistresses, and all their children bastards. Such an appalling insult to Indian womanhood, especially in a still highly traditional community, provoked moral outrage. Women crossed the frontier to the Newcastle coalfields in Natal and their presence brought out on strike the indentured Indian miners. This was the crucial breakthrough to a popular movement involving the indentured workers who had previously eluded Gandhi's efforts. From Charlestown, on 6 November 1913, the largest group of satyagrahis yet – more than two thousand – crossed the frontier into the Transvaal, and headed for Tolstoy Farm. Their mass arrest and entrainment back to

Durban for imprisonment was the triumphant climax of satya-graha. Meanwhile some 50,000 miners had gone on strike. Gandhi then displayed another dimension of satyagraha: he called off a second mass march in order to spare the government embarrassment during a strike of white railway workers. The essence of satyagraha was to claim the moral advantage.

Smuts capitulated. The Indian Relief Act of 1914 withdrew the requirement for Indians to register and carry passes; the £3 tax was abolished; the system of indenture was to cease; mar-riages were recognized; but immigration constraints remained, both between states and into South Africa. It was, after all, a compromise.

Historians have yet to do justice to the encounter between Gandhi and Smuts during these years. There remains a generally received opinion that Gandhi, in challenging the Afrikaaner, was in fact up against an opponent of a far more rigid and intran-sigent character than that of the British in India. This, it is claimed, ultimately explains the greater success of satyagraha in India.

Smuts was not a typical Afrikaaner, but on the issue of race he was far more the representative of his people. This becomes very clear if one reads Hancock's (1962) account of Smuts's long debate with Merriman, the Prime Minister of Cape Colony, in which Smuts refused to incorporate the Cape coloured franchise into the Act of Union. Neither Smuts's son nor Hancock adequately describe the encounter between Gandhi and Smuts – two outstanding moralists; maybe they cannot bring themselves to acknowledge the higher moral calibre of Gandhi. Smuts had every cause to feel considerable impatience with Gandhi. At a time when he was confronted by seemingly far more threatening social questions – the growing unrest of the poor whites, black resistance and the immense challenge of giving shape to the Act of Union – the protest of the Indian minority was a tiresome distraction. It was Gandhi's genius to force him to recognize that great issues underlay the Indian protest. Gandhi no doubt warmed to Smuts for his religious conviction, his philosophical ideas and, perhaps most of all, for his successful campaigns for prohibition and against prostitution. Yet they never really trusted one another. They were two outstanding leaders at a kind of crossroads. Smuts had come to terms with capitalism and was ready to link up the interests of a traditionalist Boer farming community and the English capitalist mining interests; Gandhi

27

was on the road to rejection of such modernization. Smuts was increasingly drawn into the maelstrom of modern power politics; Gandhi was feeling a growing alienation from the politics of power. Both men laid claim to a special vision of what civilization should be, but Smuts's vision failed to incorporate the non-whites; Gandhi's precluded industrialization. Perhaps some such narrowing of vision is essential if a moralist is to remain loyal to his or her own special vision of the truth.

Manifold influences, many discussed already, had shaped Gandhi's strategy of satyagraha. Pyarelal (1980) interestingly draws out the influences of the Boer War itself on Gandhi's thinking. To Gandhi it was a heroic struggle by an oppressed people against the empire, leading in the end to the magnanimous granting of self-government. Gandhi sought a like-minded militancy and had similar expectations of wresting moral concessions, but through the means of non-violence. Initially, Gandhi had been highly impressed by the courage of the suffragettes, especially those who courted arrest and went on hunger strikes. He was, however, to turn away from their recourse to more violent acts of vandalism. Men, he felt, should be ashamed to be shown such acts of courage by women. There was a certain male chauvinism in Gandhi's desire to replace this concept of passive resistance linked to a female struggle, by his own, satyagraha. It was only at this stage that he read H. D. Thoreau's essay 'On the Duty of Civil Disobedience' and found, in this description of the refusal by an American in July 1846 to pay tax to a state that supported slavery and his readiness to undergo imprisonment (in fact but for a day!), a distant affirmation of his own campaign.

There was a continual debate in Gandhi's mind on the manliness of non-violence. It is difficult not to link this to the decision he finally came to in 1906 to adopt a vow of celibacy – brahmacharya. It was in *Indian Opinion*, 11 August 1920, that he made a very significant statement: 'Where there is a choice between cowardice and violence, I would advise violence' (Ashe, 1968 p. 112). This question will have to be followed up further in the account of civil disobedience in India, but it should be stressed that it was central to Gandhi's view of non-violence that it was not protest by the weak but by the strong.

How to measure the success of satyagraha in South Africa? In the short run Gandhi had wrought considerable unity among the disparate, pluralist South African Indian community, each group holding to its independent traditions. Pyarelal saw in the Indian Ambulance Corps of 1899 and 1906 the promise of such unity, both for South Africa and India: 'a microcosm of all classes and creeds . . . Hindus, Muslims, Christians and Sikhs, Madrasis and upcountrymen, free Indians as well as indentured labourers' (1980, p. 276). But rifts could appear all too disarmingly. Gandhi's mission to London in 1907 was certainly weakened by a counter-petition signed by the leader of the Indian Christians and supported by colonial-born Tamils who branded Gandhi an agitator and dissociated themselves from his leadership. Throughout his South African years Gandhi was seeking a way of bridging the gap between communities, be they religious, regional or caste. In the short term he gained a considerable measure of success. Whether or not Gandhi had provided adequate policy guidance for a minority community in terms of its long term adjustment to South African politics and society is another issue: maybe it is more appropriate to consider this in terms of Gandhi's legacy (chapter 7). The seeming failure to open out the Indian struggle to embrace the interests of other oppressed groups in South Africa, coloureds and Africans, is a far more damaging point to make on the limitations of his struggle in South Africa.

Gandhi had seen racialism in South Africa as mere colour prejudice, something 'quite contrary to British traditions and only temporary and local' (Gandhi, 1927, p. 105). In fact, Gandhi was at loggerheads with apartheid in its formative phase, but he had no sense of the future structural implications for society in South Africa.

On 18 July 1914 Gandhi set out for Southampton, ostensibly to meet Gokhale and return to India together. He arrived in England two days after the outbreak of war, but Gokhale was stranded in Paris, and although the two did meet later, Gandhi returned to India alone on 9 January 1915. The years in South Africa had equipped him with an entirely new method of political struggle; how could he bring this to bear on the empire in India? His economic and social values had also undergone a profound change, and the farm communities he had set up near Durban – Phoenix Farm in 1904 and Tolstoy Farm near Johannesburg in 1910, inspired in part by his visit in 1895 to the Trappist monastery, Mariann Hill, at Pinetown outside Durban – were symbolic of a new philosophy that was now to be tested in Indian society.

3   Gandhi and the Indian Freedom Struggle: Swaraj or self-rule

The key concept in Gandhi's leadership of the Indian freedom struggle is 'swaraj'. It can be translated literally as self-rule: 'swa', one's own, 'raj', rule. Gandhi had not invented the concept but he had already, in *Hind Swaraj* (Indian Home Rule), given it his own idiosyncratic interpretation. In his eyes the overwhelming majority of Indians had not fallen under the influence of Western civilization. Village India had evaded the legal and administrative institutions and values of the cities; 'the common people lived independently and followed their agricultural occupation. They enjoyed true Home Rule' (Gandhi, 1963, p. 38). Thus a mental state of detachment was all that was necessary to achieve self-rule: 'if man will only realize that it is unmanly to obey laws that are unjust, no man's tyranny will enslave him. This is the key to self-rule or home rule' (p. 49). Gandhi's battle was to be with India's westernized elite, as the peasants were seen as natural followers of his ideals.

A quite extraordinary story was about to unfold in that a subcontinent was to undergo a vast experiment in Gandhian values. Gandhi saw in the Indian freedom struggle the greatest of his 'experiments with truth'. In his mind the political struggle was inseparable both from the economic and social and from the communal questions. Gandhi launched satyagraha in India with equal concern for economic values, for example to promote khadi, home-produced, hard-spun cloth, for social reasons, for example his attack on untouchability, and for Hindu–Muslim communal harmony. It is even tempting to claim that at the outset Gandhi felt India did not deserve freedom until such economic and social ideals had been achieved. Gandhi's thinking aloud confessional style, his working out still unformulated ideas in public, led to endless ambiguities and paradoxes, but freedom was one absolute ideal. He declared in 1931:

> The object of our non-violent movement is complete independence for India – not in any mystic sense but in the English sense of the term – without any mental reservation. I feel that every country is entitled to it without any question of its fitness or otherwise. As every country is fit to eat, to drink and to breathe, even so is every nation fit to manage its own affairs, no matter how badly . . . The doctrine of fitness to govern is a mere eyewash. Independence means nothing more or less than getting out of alien control. (Quoted by Mira Behn, 1960, p. 143.)

The interdependence of political, social and economic and communal questions in the mind of Gandhi poses awkward choices of organization for the historian. Dealing with these themes separately may be an easier way to understand the manifold complexities of modern India between 1915 and 1948. Let us therefore begin with the political struggle.

The Nature of Nationalist Protest

There were three main waves of nationalist protest: 1919–22, 1927–32 and 1939–42 (The last of these will be studied in chapter 6). The struggle for independence became the crucial example for any such struggle against imperialism throughout the Third World. At the very heart of the Indian story were the roles of violence and non-violence.

The study of history thrives on controversy, and the interpretation of the Indian nationalist movement has attracted its due share. At one stage the story was portrayed in terms of a struggle between empire and nationalism, with a wide spectrum of opinion between those who saw the virtue of empire and those who saw the nationalists as engaged in a heroic and self-sacrificing struggle. In the recent past such simplicities have been jettisoned by some historians in favour of a far more complex, more morally neutral, essentially Namierite view of Indian politics, of the struggle as one for the rewards of power. This is a highly sophisticated attempt to make sense of the way Indian society, with all its different castes, regions and communities, responded to the constitutional changes that the

British Raj introduced, from the Councils Act of 1861 and the local Government Act of 1884 onwards. As will become apparent, these changes posed difficult choices for Indians; in many ways they found themselves the victims, if often willing ones, of the political engineering of the Raj. The school of historians who have advanced this interpretation may, for convenience, and with some accuracy, be entitled the Cambridge South Asian school, whose leading spirit was above all Eric Stokes, though his field of study was the nineteenth rather than the twentieth century. Judith Brown has tested this approach on Gandhi's career (1972, 1977) and has also gone on to present this interpretation in a rather more attractive guise in her textbook *Modern India: the Origins of an Asian Democracy* (1985). As the title suggests, we are encouraged to see India's political developments less in terms of the machinations of the Raj and more in terms of the beginnings of parliamentary constitutions in the subcontinent.

Other historians, however, are reasonably distressed at the seeming exclusion of idealism from the Indian nationalist movement and the over-emphasis of the role of political factors at the expense of the economic and social. If this is not exactly an 'Oxford' view, Oxford trained historians have challenged this approach. In his study of the United Provinces (so-called as it linked parts of the former N.W. Provinces with Agra and Oudh, incorporating the great cities of Allahabad (the capital), Lucknow and Agra; it is today's Uttar Pradesh) in the inter-war period, Gyanendra Pandey, for example, claims that 'if institutional changes and the non-cooperation movement are seen as two independent points of departure for a study of the political scene in UP in the 1920s, it is quite clear that the second was the more significant' (1978, p. 27). Tapan Raychaudhuri's article (1979) attacks the Cambridge school for its excessive emphasis on self-interested politics and lays far more stress on the idealistic, on the radical and revolutionary tendencies in the Indian nationalist movement; other historians (see in particular the essays in *Subaltern Studies* edited by Ranajit Guha (1982/3)) have gone on to focus on the autonomous movement of protest by the peasantry.

It is difficult not to share in the quest for the restoration of the old simplicities of empire and nationalism; historians should never lose sight of the profoundly humiliating character of colonialism. Perhaps non-Indian historians fall into various kinds of intellectual traps in their endeavour to grasp the seemingly baffling complexities of Indian society. Raj officialdom did so by imposing all kinds of rigid divisions on Indian societies through its decennial census: maybe the Cambridge school has fallen into an analogous error of an overschematic and artificial approach. Only those from within this society could grasp its more natural inner workings and capture some of the more elementary spontaneous currents of Indian political life. Nevertheless, nationalism was an idea alien to the cultures of the sub-continent and had to be imported. There are no simple answers, and we should value all attempts at unravelling the complexities of the Indian freedom struggle.

Gandhi always differentiated between persons and institutions. If the British Empire was ostensibly his enemy, it was as a system of control: he had no particular animosity towards British people. Europeans were always to be among his closest colleagues. He had made friends easily enough on his first visit to London with members of the Vegetarian and Theosophical societies. In South Africa many Europeans were associated with his campaigns, particularly South African Jews such as the lawyer Henry Polak. Two English people were to become particularly close to him during the freedom struggle – the missionary Charles Andrews and Madeleine Slade. Charles Andrews came into contact with Gandhi through the struggle over Indian indentured labour: they first met in Durban in January 1914. Andrews had gone to India in 1904 to join the missionary staff of St Stephen's College, Delhi, and was to form friendships with several outstanding Indians besides Gandhi; Swami Shraddhanand, the Hindu ascetic and leader of the Arya Samaj, and Rabindranath Tagore, for example. Madeleine Slade (named Mira Behn, Beloved Sister, by Gandhi) was the daughter of an English admiral who, at one stage of his career, was Commander-in-Chief of the East India Station. She came to Gandhi through the spiritual pursuit of some intellectual or moral force in her life and it was in response to this vocation that she joined him in 1925 in his ashram at Sabarmati, Ahmedabad. Both Andrews and Slade were privileged English people with access to the Establishment: Andrews certainly had close contact with Lord Hardinge, Viceroy between 1910 and 1916. Maybe Gandhi saw special merit in having such English people close to him if he was to fathom the mind of the Raj. Both were to become excessively dependent on Gandhi and he was often forced to send them

33

away, Andrews to continue his struggle on behalf of Indian labour overseas, and Mira Behn to embark on various aspects of Gandhi's constructive work on her own account. Mira Behn's relationship with Gandhi was saddening and stressful. Her autobiography (1960) is one of the most unfairly neglected accounts of Gandhi's life in India.

If it was the Raj, then, with whom Gandhi's quarrel lay, one of the issues of the historiographical debate on nationalism concerns the very power of that administration. The Cambridge school has tended to emphasize its relative weakness (only matched by that of the Congress itself, certainly in its early stage). Maybe this is not a fair assumption, but it does raise the question of just how soft a target the Raj was for Gandhi's peculiar tactic of satyagraha.

In retrospect it seems obvious that fragilities would appear in the imperial system of so small an island community, indeed it was clearly at risk by the time of Gandhi's return to India in 1915. The executive weight of the empire in India rested on that 'steel-frame', the Indian Civil Service (ICS). This was an all-India administration, providing executive officers in the provinces, above all district officers and magistrates, and monopolizing most of the senior posts in its various administrative branches, the secretariat, the judiciary, the political department (responsible for the Indian princely states), and provincial governorships. As late as 1919 Europeans still held 90 per cent of its posts. However, the British middle class could not meet these demands indefinitely, and it was becoming increasingly unacceptable that talented Indians should be denied their share of these posts. In 1919 for the first time the ICS examination was held concurrently in London, Delhi and Rangoon. The Lee Commission of 1923 recommended that within 15 years half the ICS posts should be held by Indians. In fact the balance had tipped the other way by the 1930s and the rapid decline in British recruits is seen by some historians as a determining factor in the surrender of empire.

The Raj had long since recognized its dependence on Indian support: the provincial services that backed up the all-India ICS had become almost entirely Indianized in the course of the nineteenth century. Quite clearly Gandhi held a powerful weapon in his hand in calling on such Indian personnel to question their loyalty to the Raj and to respond to his patriotic appeal for non-cooperation. A similar argument might also be raised about the

Indian Army. If the Army was the ultimate sanction of British rule in India it was Indian in its composition by a ratio of two to one, and if Gandhi rarely put its loyalty to the test, others were readier to do so, as the history of the Indian National Army during the Second World War shows. According to the Cambridge school, it was this very shakiness of its executive structures that led the Raj to seek out new collaborators, and it was this that explains its constant experimentation in political forms from the 1880s onwards. It is worth emphasizing the small numbers of Europeans in India. The ICS was itself but a thousand strong; in 1931 there were 168,000 British-born or European people in India, although one might add 138,000 Eurasians or Anglo-Indians.

Gandhi returned in 1915 to an India in which the Raj was being forced to reconsider its policies. Although some Indians prospered from these war-time demands, many suffered, as inflation rose and living conditions declined. The Secretary of State for India, Edwin Montagu's famous declaration of 20 August 1917 was a promise of change:

> The policy of H.M. Government, with which the Government of India are in complete accord, is that of the increasing association of Indians in every branch of the administration and the gradual development of self-governing institutions with a view to the progressive realization of responsible government in India as an integral part of the Empire.

The declaration was guarded: there was no mention of Dominion status, which would have brought India on a par with Canada, Australia, New Zealand and South Africa. When the Montagu–Chelmsford Reforms became law in the Government of India Act of 1918 they fell far short of radical expectations.

But 'responsible government' nevertheless pointed towards internal self-government, if at a pace determined by the British. There was to be little change at the centre: liberalization came at the provincial level in the form of diarchy, a partial introduction of responsible government. A number of elected members could now hold portfolios in the governor's executive council and were responsible to the legislative council, but these were in the so-called nation-building departments such as health, education and local government; the powerful portfolios of finance and law and order were still at the disposal of the governor, though they could be held by Indians. The governor still exercised wide discretionary or reserve powers, which seemed to cancel out these limited measures of self-rule. Yet the reforms did force a change of role on officials: the ICS now found themselves working for Indian ministers. It was, however, a bad time to introduce the reforms, as the younger and more receptive officials had been drafted into the army and the old guard were antipathetic to such changes. E. M. Forster's *A Passage to India* conveys very well the mentality of senior ICS officials at this time. But Philip Woodruff (1953) and others have shown that younger ICS recruits proved responsive to the new arrangements and came to see themselves as engaged in a long term preparation of India for independence. For Indians, however, this was still seen as an insulting system of tutelage.

The lie was seemingly given to a Liberal or Whig view of such developments by the simultaneous introduction of the Rowlatt Act, containing measures to retain in peacetime widespread powers of arbitrary arrest and detention without trial as a check to the threat of terrorism. How was Gandhi to respond to such offerings?

At one level, as the Rudolphs have tried to demonstrate in a highly regarded study (1967), Gandhi may have been seeking a new psychological response to British rule. His constant emphasis on manhood and courage can be seen as a riposte to the British tactic of dividing up Indians into 'martial' and 'non-martial' races and branding the latter, which especially included the Bengalis but also the merchant bania caste, as effeminate and cowardly. Gandhi's frank exposure of the way he sought to overcome his own weaknesses, his shyness, his inarticulateness, by such means as experiments in diet, his vow of celibacy, etc., would be read by Indians as indications of strength. In this view Gandhi is seen as trying to rearticulate a kshatriya warrior ethic. It is an intriguing theory, although it may exaggerate the extent of Gandhi's concern with the rhetoric of the Raj.

Gandhi's immediate task was to alter the outlook of India's political elites, above all that of the Indian National Congress, and the years 1915–22 were those in which Gandhi made a successful bid for a truly national 'all-India' leadership. This entailed both profound debate on policy and a major overhaul of party organization, although this still did not leave Gandhi in certain control of the nationalist movement. However, it is a mistake to see Gandhi as constantly at the centre of the stage and directing events, because it was only on rare occasions of national upheaval that he could impose his leadership. He was but one of several powerful personalities on the Indian political scene. He represented only one region in a sub-continent riven by regional rivalries. It will help to describe the policy and organizational questions confronting Gandhi, in particular in his relationship with the Congress Party, before resuming the narrative to give an account of the political struggle between 1918 and 1922.

Gandhi and the INC

The Indian National Congress, founded in 1885, was one essential political organization through which India was to achieve independence. It had split at its congress at Surat in 1907 into so-called Moderates and Extremists, characterized by Gandhi in *Hind Swaraj* as 'the slow party' and 'the impatient party'. The division had been prompted by the violent events that followed the partition of Bengal in 1905, but derived from a longer-running debate among the leadership, particularly between the two men from Maharastra province, the Chitpavin brahmins, Gokhale and Tilak, on the role of violence in the movement. (Terrorism attracted a following in Bengal, Punjab and Maharastra.) It was a debate that anticipated many of the constituents of Gandhi's own analysis of the question.

Tilak, in his commentary on the *Gita*, had sought to separate out means from ends and use this as justification for violence. In the Marathi journal *Kesari*, in 1897, he had justified the murder by Shivaji, a militant Marathi hero of the seventeenth century, of Moghul Afzak Khan. Tilak was linked with violent resistance to Raj officialdom's control of the bubonic plague in Poona in 1897, which led to the assassination of two officials. He was charged with incitement and sentenced to 18 months' imprisonment. Tilak was again implicated in terrorist outrages, this time in Bengal, and in 1908 was sentenced to six years' imprisonment in Rangoon. This 'martyrdom' made Tilak into far the greatest alternative leader that Gandhi had to confront on his return to India. Indeed, Gandhi while in South Africa not only brooded on such events in India but, on a visit to London, had to argue the case against terrorism with extremists. It is possible that the memory of the murder of Sir William

Curzon-Wyllie, an India Office official in London in 1909, intensified his challenge to the extremists in *Hind Swaraj*. Gandhi's was a new version of the means versus ends debate. 'Brute force' was seen as part of European civilization in India and if Indians sought to evict the British by such means they would still be left under the sway of an alien culture and would not become free. He had in mind D. V. Savarkar, a Tilakite who had been found guilty of incitement in London, when he elliptically concluded his *Hind Swaraj*: 'he will understand that deportation for life to the Andamans is not enough expiation for the sin of encouraging European civilization' (1963, p. 64).

Yet Gandhi's position on violence was not absolute. He was in constant dispute with the defendants of violence: Congress, for example, came close in 1929 to defending the terrorist Bhagat Singh, who had assassinated an official in Lahore, and there were many moments when Gandhi feared he might lose this battle. But he was in no way self-righteous; each position had to be tested on the anvil of experience. Francis Hutchins (1973) sees Gandhi jostling between various positions: non-violence might prevail over violence, but violence would win out over cowardice; violence might be justified where it was spontaneous and not premeditated, used in self-defence rather than aggression. This may be to anticipate an interpretation of 1942, but his position may have been more circumstantial than has generally been perceived to be the case.

Yet it was Gandhi's confrontation with the Moderates within the INC which posed an even more radical challenge to the party's leadership. His was now an invitation to men whom he admired, and had once imitated, to follow his own example of self-denial and asceticism. In South Africa Gandhi had pursued a very similar professional career to that of the early leadership of the Congress. Many were, like him, sons of minor officials whose professional careers had brought an affluence and lifestyle well beyond those of their fathers, together with a strong acculturation to Western values. Gandhi had given up his own exceptionally prosperous legal practice in Durban and Johannesburg convinced, as he powerfully argued in *Hind Swaraj*, that the practice of law in the English courts was mere parasitism on clients and a fundamental cause of Indian enslavement to British values. However, it was not merely such Indian involvement with European professions that he rejected; it was the entire political philosophy that was seen to go with it – subscription to British constitutional practice, to the politics of bargaining and petitioning. Gandhi signalled this rejection through the symbolism of clothes, exchanging his European dress for the dhoti of the Indian labourer and returning to India dressed as a Kathiawadi rustic. This was to challenge the very man he had seen as his political guru, Gokhale, the leading exponent of such a liberal, parliamentary and gradualist approach in the Indian National Congress, and Gokhale's death in 1915 may have spared Gandhi an unusually difficult and painful showdown.

Gandhi was now going against the grain of far more powerful tendencies in Indian elite politics than terrorism, for Indians did largely subscribe to English constitutional measures and were all too ready to participate in the new institutions, from the local boards at rural and municipal level initiated in 1884, to the provincial legislative council and the central legislative assembly, a broadening of the political process furthered by the reforms of 1918. Participation had been the preferred policy of the first generation of Congress leaders and was to be continued by a would-be second generation, men such as T. P. Sapru, Jayaker and Srinivasa Sastri, who after 1918 were forced to cut their links with Congress because of Gandhian policies and form the National Liberal Party. Jinnah was another key representative of this Moderate tradition, whose career is discussed below. Parliamentarianism remained a powerful element within the Indian National Congress and Gandhi found himself in constant debate with those who were anxious to join the representative bodies, whether to attack the Raj from within or to profit from such bodies as best they could. Gandhi's revolt against such forms of government set him increasingly apart from those strands of opinion, but he was too much the democrat himself to rule them out, out of hand.

Possibly the greatest stumbling-block to Gandhi's policies lay in the deficiencies of the INC as a political organization. Its limitations were many: language for example – it conducted its affairs in English when only one per cent of British India's population of 244 million in 1911 were literate in English. It was limited by social composition: it was predominantly Brahmin and high caste and this elite was, besides, overwhelmingly Hindu rather than Muslim. Its membership was largely based on the capitals of the oldest provinces, Calcutta, Bombay and Madras, reflecting above all the long-term involvement of some Indians with the British presence in India. It lacked both any strong

39

executive machinery and any extensive provincial networks. To counter this, at the Nagpur Congress of 1920 Gandhi introduced reforms to create a more powerful executive, with a working committee of 15 in permanent session, elected by an all-India committee of 350, and a network of committees at provincial, district, taluq and village level – or such was the plan – thereby transforming the Congress into a structure with genuine claims to be an all-India organization. Above all, this was an attempt to reach beyond the elites to the peasantry; to reach from urban to village India.

Gandhi set about building up his own power-base in India with considerable acumen. It was a question both of establishing a new provincial base and attracting politicians to his cause, often men from the up and coming provinces of the sub-continent rather than from the traditional centres of Congress power. His political base was to be the Sabarmati ashram in Ahmedabad, capital of Gujarat, and it is worth considering at the outset how far Gandhi saw himself as a champion of his home province. At that time, of course, no such province existed: the future province of Gujarat was still embedded in the Presidency of Bombay and neighbouring princely states. But Gandhi was a Gujarati: he wrote in Gujarati and sought influence through his Gujarati journals, like Navavijan. The dialogue form of *Hind Swaraj* was a reflection of Gujarati literary convention. At the first Gujarat Political Conference, 2–5 November 1917, Gandhi signalled his attempt to break away from the Congress bosses in Bombay by insisting that all speeches should be in Gujarati: Jinnah attempted to conform, but Tilak insisted on speaking his native Marathi.

The use of vernacular languages was both an attack on the use of English by the Congress elites and a critical step in activating a new following behind the Congress, both in those provinces subject to recent political mobilization by the Congress party and from far broader strata of the population. A by now familiar argument emphasizes the way Gandhi turned to so-called backward provinces, such as Andhradesa in the south, in an effort to outmanoeuvre the party power centres in Calcutta, Bombay and Madras. He also attempted to strike up an alliance with growing Congress power in the United Provinces and Bihar, a move away from the maritime cities which the Raj had brought into prominence and towards the traditional heartlands of power in India – the Gangetic plain. (The Raj itself had already decided on a similar move with its decision in 1911 to change the administrative capital from Calcutta to Delhi.) It was from these newly mobilized areas that Gandhi drew many of his followers: the prosperous Ahmedabad lawyer, Vallabhai Patel; Rajendra Prasad from Bihar; and C. Rajagopalachari, 'the conscience of Gandhi', admittedly from Madras, but originally a country (mofussil) lawyer in provincial Salem; and, most significantly, the Nehrus, father and son, from Allahabad in the United Provinces.

Gandhi's moral influence on these followers was astonishing. They were all men who might have pursued successful professional or administrative careers. Most striking maybe was the conversion of Motilal Nehru, a highly Westernized lawyer, who proved ready to throw over the habits of a lifetime, join his son Jawaharlal in the wearing of khadi and accept Gandhi's policy of non-cooperation. Patel and Rajagopalachari likewise made considerable sacrifices in following Gandhi's leadership.

Although Gandhi had returned to India as a national hero and had not lost touch with Indian politics during his South African years, he had still to find his way in a land as yet unfamiliar to him. The man who could have advanced his political career, Gokhale, died suddenly on 19 February 1915 but Gandhi remembered and took his advice to take a vow of silence for a year and rediscover India. Tilak, the Extremist leader, had returned to the scene, much subdued following his detention in Rangoon, but in 1916 he started up a Home Rule League. Annie Besant had started a parallel League in 1915. It was a symptom of how fragile the claims of Congress were to being a national party, that an English woman like Annie Besant with no knowledge of vernacular languages, could achieve high office in the Congress party. She was to be its president in 1917. Gandhi encouraged the return of Tilak to power, perhaps hopeful that he had rejected violence, and in 1916 old scores between the Moderates and Extremists were settled at the Lucknow Congress. Meanwhile Gandhi had set up his base at Sabarmati on 20 May 1915 and from there, as much in response to demand as through any initiatives of his own, initially engaged in both peasant and urban worker struggles in Champaran, Kaira and Ahmedabad. (These will be discussed in the next chapter.) At this time Gandhi had still to disengage himself from empire and he acted as much outside Congress as within. It was the Rowlatt Act of 1918 which provided the catalyst to a still tentative political career as a nationalist in the sub-continent.

41

The Rowlatt Bills, with their powers of arbitrary arrest and detention without trial to defeat terrorism, provided Gandhi with an ideal challenge for testing out satyagraha for the first time in India in a political context. It was a strategy that worked best against a very specific issue: the Rowlatt Acts were clearly analogous in this respect to the Black Act of the Transvaal. A satyagraha sabha association was set up in Bombay on 24 February 1919, following a meeting at Gandhi's Sabarmati ashram. A vow was to be taken to refuse to obey the laws should they be implemented. By mid-March some 600–800 people had signed the pledge within the Presidency of Bombay. Quickly the Indian liberals in the Central Legislative assembly and Mrs Besant signalled their disapproval. Relying on his inner voice, Gandhi adopted a traditional mode of protest, a hartal, or a day of shutting up shop and giving the day over to fasting and prayer, to inaugurate satyagraha on 6 April. This was not in itself an act of civil disobedience. On 7 April Gandhi infringed restrictions on the sale of forbidden literature by selling openly, amongst other tracts, *Hind Swaraj*. On 8 April he left Bombay to organize satyagraha in Delhi and Amritsar but the government, rightly alarmed by his protest, confined him to the area of the Bombay Presidency. News of his 'arrest' led to far more violent protest in his own city of Ahmedabad on 10 April and in Amritsar, in the Punjab, a violent confrontation was to occur which had a lasting impact on the politics of the sub-continent.

On 13 April 1919 some 10,000 (this is the higher figure quoted) unarmed Indians had gathered in Amritsar in an enclosed space, known as the Jallianwalla Bagh. Not all were there out of loyalty to Gandhi's satyagraha protest; some were simply agitators and the largest number were those who had come to attend the annual horse fair and were unaware of either the Gandhian protest or the ban on public meetings. It was on this crowd that Brigadier-General Dyer, a British Army officer in the Punjab, gave the infamous orders for his troops to fire. They continued to do so for some 10–15 minutes: 379 of the crowd were killed, 1,200 wounded. The market place became a death trap as the terrified citizens found the exits blocked. Ill-informed of the events in Amritsar and disturbed by the conduct of protesters in his home city, Gandhi gave way to self-blame and accused himself of a 'Himalayan blunder' in launching satyagraha prematurely. On 18 April civil disobedience was suspended and on 21 July, satyagraha likewise. The government lifted its confinement order on Gandhi on 15 October.

India in 1919 was on the brink of revolution. Such was the economic distress and the political expectation bred by the country's war-time sacrifices that events in Ireland and Russia seemed all too relevant to colonial India. Gandhi resumed his campaign, but this time rather more, though not exclusively, through Congress. Gandhi's aim was to lead the Congress towards a boycott of the assembly elections set for November 1920, although, in his usual way, he had moved intuitively towards his decision. As the full enormity of Dyer's conduct in Amritsar dawned more and more on Raj and Congress alike, Gandhi made himself increasingly indispensable to Congress by the leading role he played in drawing up Congress's own report on the 'Punjab wrongs'. The report was published on 25 March 1920: the official government Hunter Committee Report came on 28 May. The revelation that Dyer had resorted to massacre as a deliberate measure to intimidate the Punjab into acquiescence – the authorities were additionally afraid of an Afghan invasion – exposed the worst aspect of the government's handling of the crisis; but it was the subsequent reaction in England, with the House of Lords rejecting the House of Commons' censure of Dyer's conduct and the distasteful racism that the response to the Amritsar massacre revealed, that did more to antagonize Congress and resolve Gandhi's own ambiguities about non-cooperation. Gandhi insisted that the Rowlatt satyagraha had not in itself been responsible for the violence.

If Gandhi drew Congress behind his leadership through his handling of the Punjab issue, at the same time he sought additional support outside Congress from the Indian Muslims, a community increasingly outraged at the Allied governments' handling of Turkey and the threat this posed to the spiritual powers of the Turkish Sultan as Caliph of Islam. The details of the Khilafat movement will be considered in chapter 5: here it is sufficient to show how Gandhi opportunistically drew on another issue to orientate Indians towards a renewal of civil disobedience. Gandhi was now set to try out satyagraha on an entirely new scale. No longer was it tied to a specific grievance, but to a cause – that of Swaraj.

The campaign was to be in several stages, instituted by Gandhi's own call for non-cooperation on 1 August 1920. He was asking Indians to withdraw support from the Raj at many levels: from the civil service, the law courts, government schools and, above all, from the newly constituted legislative councils. It was a tall order to ask Congress to boycott the greatest prospect of political power the Raj had yet offered, but Gandhi's will prevailed in the Special Calcutta Congress in September. Perhaps Motilal Nehru's conversion to non-cooperation was the key to his success. Gandhi went on to impose his leadership on the party at the Nagpur Congress in December of that year. Tilak, the one remaining Congress figure who might have challenged Gandhi's leadership, died on 1 August 1920.

Gandhi now stepped up the non-cooperation campaign by a plan for civil disobedience; the taluq of Bardoli was chosen to break the law by refusing to pay taxes. This stage was initiated in February 1922, but by then the campaign had already acquired a momentum Gandhi could no longer control. In July 1921 the Ali brothers, leaders of the Khilafat movement, had been arrested for declaring that it was wrong for Muslims to serve in the British Army: the Muslim community, bereft of leadership, was drifting increasingly into violence. Almost willingly, Gandhi seized on a violent peasant attack on a police station in Chauri Chaura, Gorakhpur (in the Eastern United Provinces) on 4 February 1922 as an excuse for calling off the civil disobedience campaign. His political colleagues were incredulous and dismayed: he seemed to have interrupted an upsurge of Indian protest in full flood. On 10 March 1922 Gandhi was arrested. Prison, it seemed, was a welcome escape from an almost impossible position.

How successful had the campaign been? Judith Brown (1972) is anxious to emphasize the limitation of Gandhi's control of the movement. Response had varied considerably, with Bombay province the most effectively politicized. The loyalty of the civil service to the Raj had not been broken: only a few civil servants, e.g. honorary magistrates, had resigned. But the Westernized elite had responded, with many lawyers ceasing to practise in law courts and many students temporarily boycotting the government schools, although such was the demand for education that Congress had to provide alternative 'national' schools. In terms of the nationalist movement, the situation had fundamentally changed. No longer could the Raj deride the Congress as a mere talking shop. John Grigg has argued in an article (1983) that

Gandhi's orientation of national protest into the channel of non-violence had played into the government's hands and that Gandhi's leadership effectively delayed independence by some 30 years. But the Raj had been severely shaken. Viceroys Chelmsford and Reading had both chosen to proceed cautiously: their main fear was that a punitive response to non-cooperation would drive the new Moderates or Liberals into the arms of Congress and so put at risk the constitutional experiments instituted by the Montagu–Chelmsford reforms. In some provinces, the Raj could point to a positive Indian response to its reforms as, for example, with the success of the Justice Party in the Presidency of Madras, but the Congress boycott remained an embarrassment. The government was forced to be increasingly sensitive to Indian public opinion for Gandhi had fundamentally altered the rules of the game. From now on there was to be a struggle between Raj and Congress for *moral* advantage and government repression would seem as much a defeat as a victory.

The government's staggering insensitivity in appointing an all-European Commission of Inquiry, led by Sir John Simon (a former Solicitor-General, Attorney-General, Home Secretary and leading Liberal politician), to investigate the workings of the Montagu–Chelmsford reforms prompted the renewal of nationalist protest in 1927. Gandhi, imprisoned for six years on grounds of sedition in March 1922, had been released in January 1924, following an appendix operation. Prison had provided the opportunity for extensive reading and in 1925 he took up the task of completing his autobiography, *The Story of my Experiments with Truth*. In the years up to 1927 Congress was torn by debate no longer on whether or not, but *how* to respond to the Montagu–Chelmsford legislative councils. Initially the debate had been between C. Rajagopalachari, defending a Gandhian no-changer position, e.g. boycott of the legislative assemblies, and the Bengali C. R. Das, leader of the Swaraj party, formally launched in 1923, but still linked to Congress, advocating the strategy of standing for election and attacking the government from within the councils. With Das's death on 16 June 1925, leadership of the Swaraj Party passed to Motilal Nehru who continued his policy. Increasingly the debate oscillated between whether to enter the councils in a Parnellite spirit of subversion or a Responsivist one of extracting such advantages as could be won from the constitutional changes. Pandit Malaviya advocated the latter tactic in the United Provinces, and it was an approach very attractive to Madras parliamentarians within Congress, such as Satyamurthi. Gandhi had little sympathy and little skill for building up such an all-India parliamentary movement, but he was too much the democrat to deny his formal approval to the Swaraj Party.

Anger at the composition of the Simon Commission prompted both protest at its presence in the sub-continent and renewal of a far more radical debate on Indian independence. The majority of Congress politicians probably remained attracted to some positive response to the councils, but a minority voice of radical nationalists, led by Jawaharlal Nehru and Subhas Bose, was impatient at all such tactics and favoured a renewal of protest on behalf of independence. A debate now ensued between the relative merit of Dominion status, advocated as the objective by Motilal Nehru in his Congress report of 1928, and the radical nationalists who sought full independence. The new Viceroy, Lord Irwin, subtly exploited these divisions by declaring on 31 October 1929 that it was 'implicit in the declaration of 1917 that the natural issue of India's constitutional progress as then contemplated is the attainment of Dominion status'. It was left to Gandhi, his own image as leader refurbished by the success of a renewed attempt at satyagraha in Bardoli taluq in 1928, to act as broker in this Congress debate and once again assert his leadership. He hedged on the issue of Dominion status rather than independence (his own preference, however, still remained for some continuing relationship with Britain), and at the Lahore Congress of 1929 he was granted full powers to decide how best India should now engage in a renewed struggle for 'purna swaraj', complete independence.

The 'inner voice' led Gandhi to choose the government's monopoly of the salt tax as the pretext for the next major satyagraha campaign. Judith Brown (1977) sees it as 'a superbly ingenious choice': it was harmless enough not to alienate the Congress Moderates but an issue of such widespread popular concern that it would mobilize a mass following. Gandhi was 'under instruction' from the Congress high command not to allow another 'Chauri Chaura' to put him off his stride, and there were signs of a greater tolerance of violence; now he would prefer 'being a helpless witness to chaos to perpetual slavery' (Brown, 1977, p. 88). Gandhi was concerned, however, to impose his will on the conduct of satyagraha and initially it was restricted

46

to those areas of Gujarat which he himself had propagandized in the 1920s. The famous salt march to Dandi, a 240 mile walk from Sabarmati to the sea, accompanied by 78 male satyagrahis, passed through taluqs that had been exposed to the values of satyagraha over several years. He set out on 12 March 1930: on 6 April at the coast he picked up a lump of mud and salt and boiled it in sea water to make salt. Initially the government left him free, but his decision to invade a salt works on 24 April led to his arrest on the night of 4/5 May 1930.

The confrontation and eventual agreement between the Viceroy Irwin and Gandhi is a high point in the history of Gandhian satyagraha. Here Gandhi faced a moral protagonist of analogous stature to Smuts in South Africa. Irwin was a deeply religious Anglican. Gandhi was to say, 'I submitted not to Lord Irwin, but to the honesty in him.' He had been a reluctant Viceroy in 1926 and his gravest error lay in his acceptance of the all-European composition of the Simon Commission, but no doubt he could have claimed that this would exclude Indian factionalism from its deliberations. He continued a Viceregal pattern of occasional meetings with Gandhi but it is doubtful whether he ever understood him: 'a most baffling enemy, generous, irrational and elusive and as hard to pin down on a point of logic as a butterfly on the plains of his native Gujarat'. He wrote, in response to the Dandi salt march: 'I was told a few days ago that his [Gandhi's] horoscope predicts that he will die this year and that is the explanation for this desperate throw. It would be a very happy solution.' Irwin's response to Gandhi was one reflection of the general paradox of English political attitudes in the 1930s. Irwin's 'tender' response to Gandhi was analogous to the appeasement approach to Nazi Germany; this was probably as half right as was Churchill's 'tough' response to both Gandhi and Hitler.

On 17 January 1931 Irwin offered Gandhi the opportunity of talks to discuss constitutional reform. The political climate had changed following the election to Westminster of a Labour administration and by 1931 the Prime Minister, Ramsay Macdonald, was in a position to offer full provincial autonomy and, with the rulers of the princely states coming into the federal executive, a central executive responsible to a federal legislature. True to the satyagraha ideal of reasonableness and responsiveness to oportunities for dialogue, Gandhi felt he had to respond to Irwin's offer. He was released from gaol on 26 January

1931. Throughout 1930 Gandhi had been particularly anxious not to alienate Jawaharlal Nehru and had rejected the blandishments of the Indian liberals for compromise out of a wish to respect Jawaharlal's radical sensibilities. But the death of Motilal Nehru on 6 February 1931 created a new psychological relationship between the two men: its father–son character was strengthened and Nehru was now more inclined to accept Gandhi's approach.

The Gandhi–Irwin talks form a bizarre episode in the history of independence, with Madeleine Slade in attendance to prepare Gandhi's meals – currently dates and milk – on an uncarpeted part of the marble floor of Irwin's study in Viceroy House. A truce was agreed by 5 March. Irwin managed to avoid conceding an inquiry into police excesses and Gandhi agreed that there would be no renewal of civil disobedience during his attendance at the Round Table Conference in London. There were many compromise measures: the government would restore land forfeited for non-payment of revenue providing it had not been sold to a third party; officials who had resigned would be reinstated providing that nobody else had taken up their post on a permanent basis; people could collect salt should they live in salt-providing areas, but only for domestic purposes. Judith Brown claims that 'the conclusion of the Gandhi–Irwin pact as it came to be known probably marked the peak of Gandhi's political influence and prestige in India' (1977, p. 191).

Yet Gandhi was inspired by ideals of immediate political change and neither the politicians he met in London, let alone Irwin's intransigent successor as Viceroy, Lord Willingdon, were in the mood to grant such reforms. Civil disobedience was renewed on 31 December 1931 but this time the government was ready. In what, in retrospect, was a dress-rehearsal for August 1942, the government ruthlessly repressed the Congress Party and Gandhi was back in gaol on 4 January 1932.

There was a strange paradox about the civil disobedience campaigns between 1929 and 1934. Gyanendra Pandey (1978) has shown how the INC itself became a much more efficiently organized structure; the Congress was transformed from a movement into a party. The foundation laid by Gandhi between 1920 and 1922 proved sound, although a major overhaul was needed between 1929 and 1931. The real breakthrough in party discipline had come at the provincial level. But civil disobedience had been caught up in social forces that it still barely understood. It had coincided with the world depression of 1929 and it was the drop in prices for primary products and the trade recession that had driven both peasants and merchants into civil disobedience. As Congress sensed these underlying social grievances it tended to move backwards in a conservative direction; after all, it remained essentially the movement of the Westernized elite. 'As the organization and strength of the Congress increased and the scale of its campaign widened, the social depth', writes Pandey, 'actually diminished'. Congress had yet to come up with 'any real analysis of the structure of imperialist domination or of the forces and contradictions within local society' (1978, pp. 195–6).

Civil disobedience was not finally withdrawn until 7 April 1934. While many Congress politicians returned once again to parliamentary politics, Gandhi was far more drawn into these challenging questions of the social base of Congress, and it is to Gandhi's ideas on India's economy and society that we must now turn.

4 The Indian Economy: Sarvodaya or social uplift

If Gandhi's ultimate ideal was social harmony, how was this to be achieved? Was Gandhi a social conservative or a revolutionary? That this remains a difficult question to answer derives largely from the constant shifting in Gandhi's thinking on economic and social issues. He tentatively thought his way into these questions on his return to India but, as he confronted the poverty and inequalities of Indian society, his thoughts became increasingly radical.

It would be mistaken, however, to try to see Gandhi in the same mould as a social radical of a modern Western society, or indeed a radical social reformer of modern India. His remained a deeply religious quest. In his view everyone's dharma or social obligation entailed seva or service. Such service was on behalf of lokasamgraha, the welfare of all, or of sarvodaya, a more familiar concept, meaning 'the rise of all'. If Hinduism is a religion that responds to suffering rather than to sin (though sin for Gandhi was also central), then Gandhi was within a Hindu tradition of social reform. Even if in the imperfect Kali Yuga, the Black Age, society was inherently imperfect, Gandhi was inspired by the traditional ideal of the Satya Yuga, the Golden Age of truth, the realization once again of the Kingdom of Righteousness, of God, on earth – Ram Rajha.

Such a vision was inextricably linked with Gandhi's pursuit of swaraj. He had inherited from the early Congress its ideal of swadeshi (economic self-reliance), a marriage of political and economic ideals. Gandhi, however, significantly altered the content of swadeshi, with its championing of Indian manufactures over imported, especially British, products. His was a vision of self-sufficiency, or autarchy, of a far more local kind. Swadeshi for him, literally meaning 'one's own locality', came to mean only using those products that came from one's own culture and one's immediate surroundings. It was a philosophy that brought Gandhi into conflict with factory manufactures, both home produced and imported. (See Chandra, 1966, for discussion of the early Swadeshi movement.)

In Gandhi's 'constructive movement', which sought to realize his economic and social ideas, the essential platforms were the use of home-spun khadi, Hindu–Muslim unity and anti-untouchability. Such specific aims sprang, however, from a wider vision of the kind of economy and society he wanted for India. However important political freedom was, its justification lay in making possible the fulfilment of this vision. Parallel to the Congress Party, volunteer organizations emerged, service bodies, seva sanghs, wedded to satyagraha and dedicated to realizing the constructive programme. But it is not enough for the historian simply to describe Gandhi's recommendations: he must also assess the degree to which Gandhi grappled with the underlying challenge of social transformation and development. This chapter will therefore concentrate on economic questions: the nature of the agrarian economy and the plight of the peasantry, the emergence of Indian capitalism and the plight of handicraft workers and of factory workers. It will be left to the next chapter to look at social questions, above all those of community and caste.

On his return to India in 1915 Gandhi quickly took up the experiment he had initiated in South Africa at Phoenix and Tolstoy Farms of lay communities or ashrams. Their history is a microcosm of that of the whole constructive movement and should be sketched at the outset. Gandhi was not the first to reformulate the traditional Hindu idea of ashrams: Gokhale, for one, had already done so in his Servants of India Society. These were not retreats from the world: they were very much part of society, experimental centres for social change. Plague drove Gandhi from his first ashram and the village of Kochrab into the centre of the city of Ahmedabad, and to the Sabarmati ashram which became his centre of operations until 1933. 'Though situated on the bank of the river and with some fields around' it did not, wrote Mira Behn (1960, pp. 90–1), 'have a country atmosphere. One looked across the river at a forest of factory chimneys, whose smoke often polluted the air; and as for walks they consisted in trudging along an uninteresting road from the Ashram gate to the gaol gate and back.' Sabarmati was a home for many satyagraha families from South Africa: it was not, in many ways, an ideal community for putting his ideas to the test. In 1915, on a visit to Benares, Gandhi had attracted a twenty-year-old student, Vinoba Bhave, later to succeed Gandhi as leader of the constructive movement; his ashram at Wardha, with its emphasis on celibacy and its absence of contentious family-life, became a more spiritual version of ashram life, and in 1936 Gandhi was to set up a second ashram nearby in the village of Sevagram. In 1931 he had taken a vow, on the eve of departure for the second Round Table Conference, that he would not return to Sabarmati till India had won independence. Later he was to argue that it was unjust that the ashram should retain its property while peasants and officials had lost theirs in the civil disobedience movement, so Sabarmati was disbanded. Initially at Wardha Gandhi lived over the Mahila Ashram, or Women's Institute, then in a comfortable building donated by Jamnalal Bajaj; but in 1936 he moved to the village of Segaon, later renamed Sevagram, and so finally came to terms with village India. Gandhi had chosen to live 'in one of the hottest places in India'. In the months of May and June he kept 'his head perpetually wrapped in a wet cloth' (Mira Behn, 1960, p. 193). But, as with all Gandhi's decisions, it was also politically inspired: Wardha was near Nagpur, at the centre of the Indian railway system, and it was a convenient rendezvous point for Gandhi and Congress politicians.

In the ashrams Gandhi was among his most loyal followers. Apart from Kasturbai, his family were not to follow him from Sabarmati to Sevagram. Common to both communities were his secretarial staff, Mahadev Desai and Pyarelal. Desai, a Gujarati, joined Gandhi in 1917 and became absolutely indispensable as his Chief Secretary: 'both his hands', as Kasturbai put it. He was to die of a heart attack shortly after joining Gandhi in detention at Poona in August 1942. Pyarelal, a Punjabi from Lahore, less well organized than Mahadev, was to succeed him as Chief Secretary and later became Gandhi's official biographer, a work unfinished, however, at the time of his own death. Gandhi was always attended by loyal female disciples (and herein lay some emotional hardship for Kasturbai) including Madeleine Slade, Sushala Nayar (Pyarelal's sister) and, towards the end, younger relations, such as his niece, Manu Gandhi. (There are vivid accounts of ashram life in Madeleine Slade's memoir and Ved Mehta's *Mahatma Gandhi and his Apostles* (1977), and of his ashram lifestyle in Eastern Bengal, 1946–7, in N. K. Bose's

My Days with Gandhi (1953). The source material for Gandhi's life is, of course, extensive.)

There was a constant emphasis on cleanliness and on punctuality and routine. Sanitation became an obsession with him, and all were expected to play their part in latrine duties (maybe easier for Gandhi than most as he had no sense of smell). The daily routine of ashram life had affinities with the monastic, with early morning prayers at 4.00 am and evening prayers. This was partly directed at inward spirituality and asceticism, most controversially in terms of brahmacharya. Gandhi's quest to master his sexual drive underlay much of his self-discipline and dietetic austerities, and his experiment of sleeping with female disciples to test his sexual self-control became a highly controversial aspect of ashram life. Yet it was based on a belief that only such sublimation would grant him the spiritual powers to cope with the demands outside, and whatever the damage to such followers as Manu Gandhi, it was in Gandhi's eyes, particularly at the end of his career, an experiment he had to undergo to prove his fitness for challenging the nightmare of communalism with its murderous war between Hindus and Muslims. The ashram was to be a model for village India, therefore its members took on all the tasks that Gandhi believed were essential for village uplift. The ashrams became training centres in making khadi; they also became testing grounds in social engineering for it was essential that these caste–Hindu communities should absorb untouchables if any example were to be set for anti-untouchability. But ashrams were also intensely political. Only the spiritual training in the ashram would equip the Volunteers for the courage and discipline required for satyagraha. The ashramites were to be in the forefront of civil disobedience.

Gandhi came to address questions of the Indian economy with no expertise in economics and none of the specialist knowledge that would be the stock-in-trade of the development economist. Gandhi was no agronomist, no demographer. He came to an agrarian economy where change over the centuries had been minimal, and perhaps it is not surprising that his focus should be on the social rather than the economic aspects of rural India. It may have been that changes in social attitudes and social structure represented the best chances of advance in so depressed an economy.

Gandhi's was an attack on extremes of poverty: in one district of the United Provinces, agricultural labourers customarily ate grain collected from the excreta of animals. The Indian economy was predominantly rural, with some 700,000 villages, wherein resided some 80 per cent of the population, the remaining 20 per cent in the urban and manufacturing sector. Gandhi seemingly fell subject to the myth of the self-sufficient Indian village, but the village was never as isolated as this supposes and would always have been locked into regional economies. But a strong anarchist impulse underlay the importance Gandhi placed on the village economy and its social order.

Historians often compare the Indian intelligentsia of the 1920s with that of Russia in the 1860s in their common quest to understand the peasantry. The Russian populists sought out the peasant in a spirit of atonement, to compensate for guilt at the long history of exploitation of peasant labour services and harsh taxation, both by the state and the aristocracy, under serfdom. Peasant indifference to such sentiment merely reinforced their sense of alienation and led to profound differences among the populists themselves as to whether they should pursue a peaceful course of propaganda and education among the peasantry or resort to a more violent attack on tsarist officialdom and landowners as the way forward towards a more just and equal society. The Indian intelligentsia were confronted by similar choices. Gandhi's was a non-violent approach, but he was forced to decide whether he accepted the current system of landownership or whether he would argue for structural change (although his answer was never entirely clear). India's was an immensely complex, multi-layered system, endlessly complicated by the widespread granting of tax-collecting and tenancy rights that had occurred under the land revenue policies of the East India Company and the Raj.

The landowning elites of India, variously known as zamindars or taluqdars, were a mixture of a traditional gentry class and new urban moneyed interests, largely Hindu. Gandhi inherited a Congress view which was broadly sympathetic to this landowning elite. As the Raj sought to contain the impact of the non-agrarian castes on the agricultural economy, through measures of debt relief and against land alienation, so the early Congress, representative as it was of the Hindu urban middle class, found itself attacking such government intervention. But neither was it at all obvious that a vulnerable Congress, anxious for financial support wherever it could be found, would necessarily turn against the traditional landowning gentry, the zamindar elite.

Gandhi initially echoed such conservatism in his concept of trusteeship which was, as we will see, a defence of property that applied equally to the industrial capitalists. The notion of trusteeship was more of a religious concept – that all land was held on trust from God – than an Indian version of feudalism, but the Indian concept of the interdependence of the different layers of a community, the jajmani system, was profoundly influential, and in part Gandhi was saying that the landowner did have reciprocal responsibilities to his tenants and agricultural workers. But he was bound to become alienated from the invariably parasitic character of the Indian landlord class, often absentee and often devoting their rental income to conspicuous consumption. If landowners failed as trustees, what right had they to transmit the land? Why should their land not be seized and redistributed to the real cultivators, without compensation? After independence legislation was quickly passed to end the special status of zamindars, if with compensation, and quite rapidly the land became held by owner-occupiers which seemed to mark the fulfilment of some radical Congress policies towards land ownership.

But the situation was in fact more complex even than this, for there were also significant class divisions within the Indian peasantry and Gandhi had to come to terms with a rural society with considerable potential for revolution. The peasantry had its own so-called dominant castes, a peasant class that formed the conservative backbone of India and increasingly came to see the Congress Party as the representative of its class interests. This group was locked in a struggle with the zamindars and taluqdars and this encouraged Congress by the 1920s to entertain its seemingly radical attack on the gentry landowning elite. Below the rich peasantry came a middle peasantry, subsistence farmers, able to make a living without selling their labour, but farmers who cultivated their own farms without the means to employ labour. Would this class see their interests in alliance with the rich peasantry or become proletarianized and join the majority of poorer peasants? The poorer peasantry themselves were a complex stratum, including those on very small farms who had to supplement their income by hiring out their service for labour, share-croppers and an increasingly larger population of landless labourers. In 1891 the landless constituted 13 per cent of the peasantry; in 1931, 38 per cent.

These class categories paralleled caste: the landless were the untouchables but also absorbed an increasing number of backward castes. To grasp the character of rural unrest one has to add to the poorer peasantry India's adivasis or tribal peoples, unevenly distributed, but numbering as many as 20 per cent of the population in Central Provinces, and 24 per cent in Orissa. These communities were likewise under increasing pressure from Hindu urban moneyed interests and oppressed by the tax demands of government, constituting another potentially revolutionary group. It was an escalation from the struggle of the rich peasantry to that of the poorer which seems to be the highest common factor in the peasant unrest of the period and it confronted Congress with a difficult decision regarding strategy. Could they risk encouraging protest among the rich peasants in the form of non-payment of rent or land revenue, if this might become the catalyst for far more extensive unrest among the poorer peasantry and the tribal peoples? How radical a vision did Gandhi himself entertain in response to the problems of this rural society?

In *Hind Swaraj* Gandhi had intimated that it was the peasants, untainted by Western civilization, who would be natural converts to his ideal of satyagraha. An appeal from a peasant from Champaran in Bihar, while Gandhi was at Lucknow in 1916, for him to take up the plight of the indigo workers, provided Gandhi with the first opportunity to put this expectation to the test. He came to Champaran in April 1917. Here he encountered a conflict between a rich tenant peasantry and a European plantocracy. With the drop in the value of indigo, the landowners had saved their own necks by commuting the required production of the crop under the so-called tinkathia system (referring to that amount of the land that had to be planted with indigo) for higher rents or a lump sum, exposing the peasants to debt through the depreciating value of their cash crop. The indigo tenants proved remarkably disciplined as Gandhi set about collecting the evidence to present their grievances. He himself successfully practised civil disobedience in his refusal to leave Champaran. The outcome was that the planters were forced to repay part of their fraudulent profits and eventually had to sell the land piecemeal to the peasants. The tinkathia system, somewhat to the relief of the planters, was phased out. Gandhi came away from Champaran convinced that the rich peasant was naturally sympathetic to non-violence.

He now became involved in peasant protest much nearer to Sabarmati, in the neighbouring taluqs of Kheda and Bardoli (David Hardiman, 1981, has ably analysed the Kheda satyagraha of 1918.) Here again the stratification within the peasantry is important: there were the rich peasants or Potidars and poorer, mainly landless, peasants, the Baraiyas and Patannadiyas. It was the Potidars who initiated protest in 1917 seeking reduction in payment of land revenue (the crop had been damaged after harvesting by fresh, late rains). Gandhi became involved by February 1918 and a satyagraha was initiated – in fact, mainly organized by Vallabhai Patel – with the rich peasants refusing to pay land revenue. If a far less disciplined protest than at Champaran, ultimately here too the peasant had the victory and the government conceded a reduction in payments. But this was only part of the story. Following the failure of the monsoon in 1918, the poorer peasantry, confronted by an increase in grain prices, resorted to a traditional protest of dadh, or dacoity, and began to loot the grain stores of both rich peasants and merchants. The Potidars, formerly themselves in conflict with the police, now turned to them for help. It was a warning to Gandhi that rich peasant protest could unleash poor peasant violence. Historians of 'subaltern studies', i.e. the history of the people rather than of the elites (see Ranajit Guha (ed.), 1982, 1983) have emphasized the extent to which this was an autonomous peasant movement. Congress was not the initiator; it merely capitalized on the appearance of unrest, often only to find it was outside Congress control and antipathetic to its own interests and policy.

Gandhi certainly became alarmed at peasant violence and subsequently insisted that peasant satyagraha should only be initiated where there had been extensive propaganda work by Congress workers and there was no risk of any escalation into violence. Such was to be the case with the satyagrahas in Bardoli, the first in 1922, called off almost at its inception following the peasant violence at Chauri Chaura, and second the successful campaign of 1928, again largely organized by Vallabhai Patel. Here was a further example of controlled protest by the Potidars. Gandhi was always reluctant to extend civil disobedience to non-payment of revenue – in 1930 it was only sanctioned after Gandhi's arrest – but he had clearly brooded on Congress's failure to communicate with the poorer peasantry and it could be argued that he chose the salt tax as the grounds of satyagraha in 1930 in a specific effort to rally their support.

This is not the place to study the increasing radicalization of peasant protest in the 1930s under the impact of the collapse of world prices in primary products. Much of the recent literature has been collected in A. Desai's *Peasant Struggles in India* (1979). All-India peasant organizations (Kisan sabhas) appeared and under the leadership of such men as Professor Ranga still tended to reflect the interests of richer peasants. But a more radical political direction was given to peasant protest by the Congress Socialist Party, set up within the Congress in 1934, and this also incorporated growing Communist contact with the peasantry. We will see later the extent to which Gandhi's evolving radicalism led to any sympathetic response to such protest, above all in 1942.

Although Jawaharlal Nehru was never formally a member of the Congress Socialist Party, he was sympathetic to its ideals, and this may be the moment for a brief digression to discuss the relationship between Gandhi and his heir-apparent, above all their differences of outlook on economic and social policy.

The young Nehru had first encountered Gandhi at the Lucknow Congress of 1916, although the turning point was not to come until Amritsar and the non-cooperation movement of 1920–2. Gandhi's idealism had provided Nehru with an escape from intolerable uncertainties. He had returned to India from a privileged education at Harrow and Cambridge in 1912; in his autobiography first published in 1936 he wrote: 'I was a bit of a prig with little to recommend me.' Born in 1889 into a wealthy Kashmiri Brahmin household in Allahabad, Nehru was trapped by privilege: his was the clasic example of the alienated anglicized intellectual, an exile in his own land. His was an impulsive romantic temperament and Gandhi's movement provided the way out of this stifling situation into contact with his own countrymen. 'The years of 1920 and 1921', states one of his biographers (B. N. Pandey, 1976, p. 77) 'were perhaps the happiest of Jawaharlal's life. He was in those years committed for the first and last time.' He came into contact with the disaffected tenant farmers of the former territories of Oudh – protest by United Provinces tenants against the taluqdars. His participation here released some pent-up conflict within himself, but he also encountered in the United Provinces a more radical peasant movement, the so-called Eke movement of poorer peasants, led by an untouchable (see the excellent analysis by G. Pandey in *Subaltern Studies*, Guha, 1982). Nehru was forced now to consider just how radical were his own prescriptions for change. The poorer peasants were attacking not just officialdom and the taluqdars, but the richer peasants as well.

In 1930–1 Nehru became more actively involved in UP tenant protest and began to chafe at Gandhi's constraints on such radicalism. It became of increasing consequence for Gandhi to retain the loyalty of Nehru, for if he could be brought into line the youth of India, spearhead of the freedom struggle, could be steered away from the attractions of terrorism and towards the tactics of non-violence. Nehru, in fact, never diverged markedly from Gandhi on the peasant issue: the real difference of outlook concerned the type of development India should pursue in modernizing its industrial sector.

The Indian economy, even if the full implications were not immediately apparent, was at a threshold of change during the First World War. In the nineteenth century India's colonial economy had been linked to the needs of the metropolitan British: it had been substantially transformed into one producing primary cash crops for export, largely to Britain, such as cotton, jute, tea and coffee, while India was also a leading importer of English manufactured goods, chiefly textiles, but also iron for railway development and public works schemes and machinery for her own nascent capitalist industry. The most conspicuous sufferers from this transformation had been the urban hand loom weavers from the great traditional centres of Indian manufacture, such as Dacca and Murshidabad. During the First World War the capacity of Indian capitalism to provide some of the textile and ordnance needs of the war economy became apparent and this led to the beginning of the end of Britain's free-trade policies towards India and the belated imposition of tariff protection for Indian capitalist interests. This marked a victory for the economic nationalism of the early Congress with its war-cry of swadeshi, and it became increasingly apparent during the inter-war period that Indian capitalists could indigenize and control India's domestic market. The conspicuous losers this time were, of course, the textile workers of Lancashire. (See Tomlinson, 1979, and Ray, 1979, for a detailed analysis of this economic change.)

Gandhi's policy was to emphasize the importance of khadi and seemingly to turn his back on industrial capitalism. His was a belated rallying to the interests of those dispossessed weavers who had drifted back to the villages to seek employment within the rural economy. Khadi became the governing obsession in Gandhi's constructive movement in the 1920s. By encouraging everyone to take up hand spinning Gandhi, at one level, was trying to convert everyone to some recognition of the redemptive value of manual labour. He was also directing the peasantry towards a way of earning a few extra annas, especially during the off-season or during famine – an answer of sorts to extreme poverty in the countryside. It was also a way of providing cotton yarn for the hand loom weavers and creating employment for village artisans. The importance of such activities to Gandhi is indicated by his setting up the All-India Village Industries Association in 1932. Gandhi included paper-making, mat-weaving, oil-pressing and manufacture of new foodstuffs among such village industries. Khadi had also, of course, a political dimension: the wearing of home-spun cloth was a highly effective way of demonstrating Congress influence. (Gandhi had even wanted the spinning of set amounts of cotton yarn to be a qualification for a category of membership (4-anna) of Congress.) Above all, khadi was that aspect of the constructive movement in which Gandhi sought to recreate a more vital village economy and create an alternative economy to that of factory manufacture and the city.

Yet here was another of those seeming paradoxes in Gandhi's career. Gandhi enjoyed exceptionally supportive relationships with Indian capitalists. In 1916 he first met the 22-year-old G. D. Birla who was to prove the most generous benefactor amongst the marwari caste merchant community of Gandhi's constructive movement and of his personal livelihood. It was Ambalal Sarabhai, Ahmedabad's leading textile magnate, who helped finance the Sabarmati ashram. One could multiply such examples of financial support from Indian capitalists.

Perhaps such backing is not so strange if one simply notes that Gandhi was a fellow bania and fellow Gujarati. But more significantly this was part of a customary relationship between India's merchant communities and its saints. Gandhi's relationship with the Birla and Sarabhai families was within a tradition of 'individualized preacher–disciple relationships' (Ray, 1979, p. 297). Their support of the constructive programme fell into a pattern of traditional charity and Gandhi was too shrewd a politician not to recognize the financial advantages of such patronage for Congress, which in part explains the conservatism of his theory of trusteeship. But it is also now apparent that the merchant communities of Bombay and Calcutta had become increasingly alert to the need to cultivate the nationalist movement, and increasingly aware that their interests were more convergent than divergent. In 1927 they set up the Federation of Indian Chambers of Commerce and Industry and in 1942 their 'Bombay Plan' betrayed remarkable similiarities of outlook to Nehru's vision for a centrally controlled economy already expressed in the Congress Planning Committee set up in 1938.

Nehru's attitude towards economic change was fundamentally different from that of Gandhi. His was a scientific education and he brought far more rational, materialist and hedonistic values to bear on the question of development. He had come under the influence of Fabianism at Cambridge but it was his visit to the Soviet Union in 1927 that ignited his idealism for some 'socialist' transformation of the Indian economy. Gandhi was able to bear with such enthusiasm, and it was through Nehru that Congress accepted the Fundamental Rights Resolution at Karachi in 1931, though these fell far short of his socialist beliefs. Yet, however impatient for change Nehru became, he was no doctrinaire socialist. He recognized that, in an underdeveloped economy such as India's, Congress had to strike up a partnership with the private capitalist sector, and his contribution to the economic programme of Congress lay less in its quasi-socialist content than in recognizing the necessity for planning. It was not Gandhi's style to gainsay those who thought differently from himself: anyway, perhaps he perceived that there was a rhetorical dimension to Nehru's vision and in practice it was not so divergent from his own. Even so, Gandhi increasingly sensed in the 1930s the danger that his ideal of a revitalized rural India might be lost sight of by a Congress backed by Indian capitalism.

One group Gandhi has been unfairly censured for neglecting is India's industrial workers. They were still a small percentage of the population, numbering some two million out of 300 million in 1939. Industrial capitalism brought all the usual hardships to India's emergent factory labour force, but it was only during the labour unrest of the First World War and after, with a growing gap between wages and the cost of living, that any trade union organization came into being. Madras gave the lead in

1918 and the All-India Trade Union Congress (nothing to do with the Indian National Congress) was formed in 1920. Nehru was elected its president for the 1929 Congress. Like all such minority movements, it was subject to constant factionalism. It split in 1929 when the right broke away to form an All-India Trade Union Federation, and it was not to come together again until 1938.

Gandhi's contribution to the trade union movement arose out of his involvement in the Ahmedabad textile strike of 1918. It was a wage strike, with the textile workers seeking a 50 per cent bonus against the rising cost of living, while the employers would only offer 20 per cent. Gandhi's instinct was for reconciliation and the context of the strike was peculiarly poignant for him as the mill-owner involved was Gandhi's leading supporter, Ambalal Sarabhai, and the leader of the workers, Ambalal's sister Anasuya. Gandhi inspired a satyagraha on behalf of a 35 per cent rise. One of the conditions of the satyagraha pledge was that the workers would not harass blackleg workers, and when this began to happen Gandhi undertook the first of his fasts. This was perhaps an unfair weapon to turn against friends, but it worked. The 35 per cent was conceded, Gandhi broke his fast and the strike was called off.

Out of the strike emerged the Textile Labour Association, in fact a federation of seven unions with the differing trades within the Ahmedabad textile factories, each forming their own craft union, linked within a federal structure. By 1939 some 60 mills and 24,000 workers belonged to the union. However, along with the Ahmedabad Labour Organization, to which it was affiliated, it stood aside from the all-India union organization. It was a labour–capital organization and reflected Gandhi's deep commitment to class reconciliation and the arbitration of disputes. Strikes were to be a last resort and it was committed to a Gandhian ideal of non-violence (see Rao, *The Industrial Worker in India*, 1939, for further information).

The ambiguities of Gandhi's attitude to labour–capital relationships was reflected in Congress policies. In the follow-up to Congress's success in the 1937 elections, Congress ministers began by courting labour and taking their side in industrial disputes: by 1938, they had switched loyalties to defending the interests of employers (see Markovits' article in *Modern Asian Studies*, 1981). The active role of the Communist Party in the trade union movement through its front organization, the Workers and Peasants Party, was a source of concern to the more moderate Congress leadership but not until 1947 did the Congress set up its own Indian National Trade Union Congress. It would be wrong to accuse Gandhi of indifference to the condition of factory workers – the extraordinary fact of his choosing to live in a leading textile city, Ahmedabad, is proof enough to the contrary – but his vision for India led him away from the cities. Urban growth threatened increasing class polarization and violence, whereas the essence of Gandhi's programme was to eradicate all class divisions through non-violent non-cooperation.

In many ways this chapter, in discussing Gandhi's concept of trusteeship, his reluctance to entertain radical peasant protest and his pursuit of labour–capital harmony, has emphasized his conservative stance. There seems to be a consistent attack on *all* forms of class conflict. In some ways Gandhi was still feeling his way towards particular grievances and moreover the whole philosophy can only be measured in association with his attitudes towards caste and untouchability. We come back to the idea that Gandhi stressed means rather than ends, particular issues rather than a totally transforming vision of a new society. But the vision of Ram Rajha was there. It is worth looking ahead to one description of his future society which appeared in his journal *Harijan* on 22 July 1946 (quoted by Chatterjee, 1983, p. 153):

Life will not be a pyramid with the apex sustained by the bottom. But it will be an oceanic circle whose centre will be the individual always ready to perish for the village, the latter ready to perish for the circle of villages till at last the whole becomes one life composed of individuals, never aggressive in their arrogance, but ever humble, sharing the majesty of the oceanic circle of which they are integral units. Therefore, the outermost circumference will not wield power to crush the inner circle, but will give strength to all within and will derive its own strength from it.

Perhaps the vision was as much a moral as an economic one, but it was one that Gandhi felt was slipping away from him by the 1930s. India was drifting it seemed, towards becoming a modern, Western, industrialized society.

5   Indian Society: Sarvodaya II

During Gandhi's lifetime India became increasingly beset by the problems of communalism and casteism. As Indian society became more intensely politicized, so ever more divisive tendencies within its richly pluralistic society became apparent. Gandhi's inner motivation to reconcile and to create social harmony led him, through the constructive movement, to reach out for the support of two communities whose uncertain loyalties did most to put Indian unity at risk: the Indian Muslims and the untouchables. Gandhi had a passionate belief in the unity of 'mother India'; to separate such communities would, in his eyes, be to inflict on Indian society a form of vivisection. If Gandhi was at different times to emphasize the importance of both Hindu–Muslim unity and anti-untouchability, these were convergent aims. The majority of Indian Muslims were converts from the untouchables and this was a quest for the closer integration of similar deprived groups with the caste–Hindu community. Indian Muslims constituted one in four of India's population; the untouchables one in five. At a time of the embryonic development of mass democracy consideration of such a large percentage of a potential democratic franchise became paramount and the political implications of Gandhi's social idealism are self-evident. Nationalism became locked with communalism in a struggle for the upper hand. It was a struggle nationalism was to lose, for with independence in 1947 came the partition of the sub-continent into the separate states of India and Pakistan. Our discussion in this chapter will cruelly and ironically expose the limitations of Gandhi's influence.

Religious toleration lay at the heart of Gandhi's philosophy of non-violence. His was an essentially pluralist view of world religions – as no religion could be certain of its own absolute claim to the truth, so all were bound to tolerate one another for fear of doing violence to the truth which each contained. It was an approach peculiarly opposed to the evangelical and the missionary. It was a state of mind that emphasized the conceptual or metaphysical side of religion, their shared quest for satya or truth, but failed to perceive that world religions are divided not by their religious insights but by the rival claims of their prophets. Perhaps the Hindu is unusually blind to this consideration as Hinduism admits to no prophets such as Buddha, Christ or Mahomet. In the twentieth century, however, as communalism spread, Hinduism did begin to 'invent' its own prophets; arguably the founder of the Hindu social reform movement Arya Samaj, Dayanand Saraswati, took on such a role and Hinduism itself increasingly acquired the character of a missionary movement.

Gandhi faced religious intolerance with his ideal of secularism. By this he meant something quite different from the Western agnostic definition; his was a concept embracing his own acceptance of religious pluralism. Gandhi, for all his interest in and borrowing from other religions, always saw himself as a Hindu. To N. K. Bose he stated: 'I have been born a Hindu and I shall die a Hindu, a Sanatani Hindu. If there is salvation for me, it must be as a Hindu. Hinduism absorbs the best in other religions and there is scope for expansion in it' (Bose, 1974, p. 85). In *Hind Swaraj* Gandhi claimed that Islam and Hinduism shared many beliefs: that just as Hindus would find many passages in the Koran acceptable to them, so the Muslims would find like passages in *Bhagavad-Gita*. If Ram was his mantra and constantly on his lips, he identified it with Rahim, a Muslim word for God. Gandhi belonged to an ancient Hindu tradition of assimilation, and something of that highly ambiguous Hindu claim to tolerance through its ability to absorb rival religions lay at the heart of Gandhi's own position and gravely impaired his claims to represent the Indian Muslims.

Communalism is an awkward phenomenon to characterize and assess. It is in no way unique to the Third World but in that context it has often been branded as a negative and anti-national force, thwarting the ambitions of Third World nationalist movements of achieving a high level of integral nationalism and unity. It is seen as politically reactionary: traditional or feudal elites exploit the loyalties of their community in order to preserve their economic and social power as a class and steer the community towards some autonomous or separate political goal which will guarantee the monopoly of administrative and political posts for themselves as that community's elite. This was very much the view that Jawaharlal Nehru was to take of the political protagonists of the Indian Muslims under the leadership of Jinnah.

Indian society was subject to a range of such communal movements, and the historian should be chary of facile generalization. One favourable interpretation of these movements would be to ascribe to them an authentic expression of nationalism and see them as indeed defending the social and cultural needs of their communities. This is arguably true of linguistic nationalism, a force which was to gain increasing strength after independence and eventually recast entirely the administrative map of India. But even if there was a separatist dimension to the movements, especially in the Dravidian movement of South India, with its quest for a separate state of Tamil Nadu, all such pressures were incorporated within the federal structure of India. The risk of political separatism became much greater, however, when the communalism was religious in origin. India might succeed in absorbing Sikh pressure for a separate state of Khalistan, but it could not resist the pressure for the Muslim state of Pakistan. Does this prove, as Jinnah was to argue, that Muslim communalism was in fact a nationalist movement? Gandhi may have temporarily deflected the pressure of linguistic nationalism into Indian nationalism by his restructuring of Congress along linguistic lines at Nagpur in 1920, but his relationship with the Indian Muslims proved far more intractable.

Responsibility for Hindu–Muslim communalism lay between the Raj and political organizations of both communities. In *Hind Swaraj* Gandhi put the blame on the British and was never entirely to shake off the comforting myth that Hindu–Muslim differences were a direct consequence of the British presence. If it were to cease, he believed these differences would disappear. The Raj made a fatal move in granting a separate electorate to the Indian Muslims in the Morley–Minto reforms of 1909, something very much in Gandhi's mind at the time he wrote *Hind Swaraj*. The Raj, of course, could always hide behind the rhetoric of empire and claim it was acting as the paternalist protector of oppressed or underprivileged communities. Until the end the Congress Party could never shake off its belief that the Raj had favoured the Indian Muslims and especially the Muslim League, using them as an instrument in its battle with Indian nationalism.

Indian Muslims had few dealings with the early Indian

National Congress. There was no particular reason why they should see in this body any means of uplift for their own community; the Raj itself was a more plausible ally. In 1906, following the partition of Bengal and the creation of the Muslim majority state of East Bengal and Assam, the first all-India political body – the Muslim League – was founded in Dacca, led by the conservative landowning elite and yet welcomed by the Westernized professional Muslims as well, who overtly looked to the Raj for the further advance of their community. The Raj responded to such loyalty by granting the separate Muslim electorate in 1909, but subsequently jeoparized this new alliance by rescinding the partition of Bengal in 1911, forcing some of the Westernized elite to recognize that quite different and anti-British tactics might be necessary if they were to benefit further the interests of their community.

Alumni of Aligarh College were to spearhead this protest, angry at their failure to win university status for the college on their own terms. The leadership came from the Ali brothers, Shaukat Ali, the elder, captain of cricket at college and sub-deputy opium agent in the administration, and Muhammad, intellectually the brighter, a failed ICS candidate but an Oxford BA in History and servant of the Baroda administration (one of India's princely states). In 1911 they had set up a Muslim University Foundation Committee, anxious to turn Aligarh into a university that would reach out to the Muslim community at large, cease to be elitist and not be under government patronage. Their failure in 1912 led them to latch on to another Muslim anxiety as a rallying cry, the fate of the Ottoman Empire and in particular of the spiritual powers of the Sultan as Caliph of Islam. This was an issue that could also win the support of the Muslim priesthood, the ulamas. Their leaders were Abdul Bari, from the Furanga Mahal seminary at Lucknow, an ardent supporter of Turkey, and another priest, Abdul Kalam Azad, a religious leader in Calcutta and editor of the radical pro-Turkish newspaper, al-Hilal. The protest movement was to initiate a new style in Indian Muslim politics, bridging the gap between the Westernized elite and the ulama, marrying politics and religion. It was a style akin to the one Gandhi himself was formulating, so it was no surprise that he should seek out the leadership of this new movement on his return to India.

If Congress were to validate its claims to being a national party it was evident that it would have to reach out to the Indian

Muslims and at all costs escape the identity of being a sectarian Hindu party. Moderates and Extremists varied in their response to this problem. The Moderates chose a path of least resistance, and by emphasizing an agnostic and secular approach to politics simply failed to impinge on the Hindu–Muslim issues. The Extremists, on the other hand, were keenly aware that only by playing on Hindu religious feelings could they break out of their confinement as a Westernized minority and become leaders of a more popular movement. Tilak was the key exponent of such a strategy, playing on historic memories of the seventeenth-century Hindu warrior Shivaji and turning Hindu religious festivals into overtly political movements. Along with other politicians of similar outlook, such as Lajpat Rai from the Punjab, he could claim that it was only from asserting such communal self-respect that Hindus could acquire strength. Muslims, he claimed, would be more likely to respect and cooperate with such a revitalized Hindu community. Tilak was answering in his way the very problem Gandhi endlessly confronted: how to renew the strength of the Indians, and give them the physical courage for the independence struggle. Tilak's solution, however, while mobilizing urban opinion behind the Extremists, led both to the antagonism of Muslims and towards violence.

An even more influential factor in arousing Hindu communalism was the Arya Samaj social reform movement, started in Bombay in 1875. Its founder was Dayanand Saraswati. Born in 1824, he came, like Gandhi, from a small princely state in Kathiawad, but his caste was brahmin to Gandhi's bania, his Hinduism Saivite not Vaishnavite, although, like Gandhi, he was to become a major social reformer, above all in his radical revision of the whole concept of caste. Dayanand increasingly played on Hindu communal concerns – the defence of Hindi against Urdu, the use of the devanigiri script instead of Arabic and, maybe most significantly of all, the defence of the cow, gaurakshini. The Arya Samaj became an influential movement throughout North India, above all in the Punjab, where Hindus were in a minority (around half the population were Muslims, three-eighths Hindu, one-eighth Sikh), reinforcing the argument that communalism was strongest amongst minority communities. In the Punjab the outstanding protagonists were Pandit Lakh Ram, to be assassinated in 1897, and Lala Munshi Ram, who took the role of holy man, or sanyassin, changing his name to Swami Shraddhanand in 1917. As leader of the Arya Samaj in the 1920s he played an important role in worsening the communal climate.

A foreboding of such discord came with the Hindu–Muslim riots of 1893. Historians must keep an open mind as to whether economic and social rather than political factors do more to explain the aetiology of communalism, but the given reasons in 1893 were religious. For a complex of reasons the cow had become a symbol for Hindus; a means of communal identity at a time of rapid change and insecurity. During the Muslim Bakr-Id, celebrated during the annual month of pilgrimage, the devout were required to sacrifice an animal in memory of Abraham's sacrifice; the cow was deemed the equivalent of seven times the value of a goat or sheep, so to cost-conscious Muslim families, who could share in the expenses of the sacrifice, the cow became an obvious choice. In 1893 widespread inter-community riots broke out over the Muslim sacrifice of cows, especially violent in Bombay, where some 200 people were killed and hundreds injured. There were to be further serious riots in the years 1907–14. Gandhi shared the Hindu reverence for the cow but deplored the sacrifice of Muslim lives in its protection. It was not as if Hindus themselves, he argued, had such a good record of caring for cows. It should be enough for Hindus to plead with Muslims to spare the cow. In South Africa Gandhi had worked with Muslims and had fashioned some sort of working relationship between the disparate Indian communities in the Natal Indian Congress and its sister organization in the Transvaal. He saw it as a major imperative to seek a similar liaison in India.

It was the protest on behalf of the Caliph, the Khilafat movement, which proved crucial in politicizing the Indian Muslim masses. As early as 1913 the Ali brothers, together with Abdul Bari, had created a society for the servants of the Ka'aba, a society to protect the holy places of Islam and the safety of Muslim pilgrims, but it was the founding of the all-India Khilafat Committee in Bombay on 20 March 1919, solidly backed by the ulamas, which took the propaganda on behalf of the Khilafat into the villages. Gail Minault (1982) has convincingly argued that for both the Westernized Muslims and the ulamas the issue of the Khilafat was more the symbol than the substance of the protest. The Westernized elite saw it as a means of rallying an anti-British movement on behalf of the Indian Muslims; the ulamas were anxious to strengthen the hold of the shariat, Islamic law, over the masses. Gandhi, however, recognized that the

Khilafat shared the nationalist ambitions of Congress and eagerly sought its alliance.

He first met Abdul Bari in Delhi in March 1918. In practice the Muslims were to set the pace: it was the Khilafat Committee which pressed for non-cooperation in August 1920, a month ahead of Congress. In 1921 they also anticipated Congress in a call for civil disobedience. Gandhi had to accept that the Khilafat leadership were not genuine converts to satyagraha; for them non-violence was merely expedient. By 1921 both the Ali brothers and the ulamas were speaking of the alternative of a violent struggle. The Greek invasion of Turkey, with the seeming connivance of Britain, led the Khilafat Committee to speak out against Muslim participation in the Indian army; they had no wish for Indian Muslims to fight against the Turks. Gandhi persuaded the Ali brothers, after his meeting with Viceroy Reading in May 1921, formally to renounce violence, but this rebounded against him when the Ali brothers found themselves exposed among their own community as cowards in deferring to the British, and Gandhi lost their trust. Eventually the government struck against the Khilafat leaders: the Ali brothers were imprisoned for a period of two years in September 1921; Azad, who took over the leadership, was sentenced to one year in December 1921. Bereft of leadership, the movement began to fall apart; later Kamal Ataturk deprived it of its rationale. In 1922 he divested the Caliph of his temporal power and in early 1924, he abolished the spiritual powers of the Caliphate as well.

But more discontent was to follow and no event was to do more to destroy the Hindu–Muslim alliance than the Moplah rebellion of August 1922. The Moplahs were a Muslim community of mixed descent, products of intermarriage in earlier times between Arab traders and the indigenous coastal people of Malabar. Some historians, K. N. Panikkar in A. R. Desai, 1979, for example, emphasize the economic and class aspects of the rising, seeing it as another example of an autonomous peasant uprising with the Moplah Muslim tenants or sharecroppers turning on oppressive Hindu landlords. The class content of the revolt is shown by the fact that the Moplah showed no animosity towards Hindu tenants or landless labourers. It was the class content of such communal violence which led radicals like Nehru to argue that the solution to communalism lay in sweeping economic and social change.

The signal for the Moplah revolt had been the desecration by police of a mosque in the village of Tirurangidi on 20 August, during a roundup of local Khilafat leaders. The ensuing violence saw the murder of some 600 Hindus and the forcible conversion to Islam of as many as 2,500 (in fact the estimated number fluctuates rather wildly and this is a maximum figure). As knowledge of the revolt circulated in the north, it became a catalyst for renewed communal violence. Between 1923 and 1928 there were, according to official government figures, 112 serious communal disorders, leaving 450 dead and some 5,000 severely injured.

While the sad details need not directly concern us, the communal organizations involved must. The Arya Samaj, under Shraddhanand, took up the plight of the Hindus; communalism was reaching out now to the Hindu majorities, greatly strengthened by a new organization initiated in 1915, the All-India Hindu Sabha, or Hindu Mahasabha. This was committed to strengthening the political awareness of the Hindu majority,. drawing on Tilak's arguments, and launched a movement known as Sangathan, which encouraged the Hindus to become more militant. The Hindu Mahasabha was a distinctly sinister movement. One of its leading theorists was G. D. Savarkar, a former terrorist released from gaol on 6 January 1924 only to become actively involved in the shuddhi movement. He was to inspire a right-wing Hindu nationalism, with fascist overtones. His biographer, Dhananjay Keer, writes: 'Savarkar felt it was his righteous duty to remove ruthlessly the web of Gandhism that had choked the political life of Hindustan' (1966, p. xx). In 1925 K. Hedgewar, a former member of the Hindu Sabha, founded the R.S.S. (the Rashtriya Swayamsevak Sabha), a para-military organization. One of its recruits was to be a chitpavin brahmin, N. V. Godse, Gandhi's future assassin.

No one was more utterly wretched at the resurgence of communalism than Gandhi. One response was the fast, the supreme weapon of satyagraha. In September 1924, while staying with Muhammad Ali in Delhi, he undertook a 21-day fast in response to the communal violence in Kohat in the North West Frontier Provinces. It prompted a Hindu–Muslim Unity Conference in Delhi, in which leaders of both communities vowed to respect both the inviolability of each other's places of worship and each other's customs. Gandhi was later unable to forgive Shaukat Ali for blaming the Kohat violence, quite rightly in point of fact, on the Hindus. Yet it was Gandhi's gamble with the Khilafat movement which had, in significant ways, contributed, if unwittingly, to the upsurge of communalism. The Congress and the Khilafat organization had never merged; they remained parallel organizations. Both the Ali brothers and Gandhi had resorted to a religious idiom in their leadership: the Ali brothers had grown beards and sported flowing green cloaks, with crescent badges, evoking the image of the maulanas or priests; Gandhi's was the political idiom of the sanyassin, the Indian mendicant saint. The Khilafat movement reached out to a mass audience but it did so in a style that heightened both Muslim and Hindu self-awareness. There may also be some truth in Erikson's argument, following Freudian theories, that Gandhi had imposed almost unbearable moral constraints on his followers, who, once the movement collapsed, were almost bound to drift into violence. Both Gandhi in the 1920s and ultimately the Raj in the 1940s were to find that one meddled in Muslim politics at great peril.

One major Muslim politician stood stonily apart from the Khilafat movement and the rupture at this stage in the relationship between Jinnah and Gandhi was one of the most costly legacies of Gandhi's encouragement of Khilafat. Born on 25 December 1876 in Karachi, and a fellow Gujarati, Mohammed Ali Jinnah belonged to the Khoja community, a sub-sect of the minority Shia community of Indian Muslims, a group exceptional in its ability to profit from the new opportunities opened up by colonialism. Through a prestige English-medium education in Karachi and Bombay and his legal training in London in the 1890s, Jinnah became highly Anglicized and was a natural recruit to the moderate wing of the Congress Party. His support for Hindu–Muslim unity and an all-India nationalism led him to reject the partition of Bengal in 1905. He only joined the Muslim League in 1913 on condition that this would not prejudice his Congress membership, and it was Jinnah, at a meeting in Bombay in 1915, where he first encountered Gandhi, who paved the way for the Lucknow Pact the following year. The condition of the pact was Congress's acceptance of separate Muslim electorates. By 1917 Jinnah stood out as a leading Indian nationalist but the non-cooperation movement and Khilafat were to all but destroy his career.

He had been elected to the Imperial Legislative Council to represent the Bombay Muslims in 1909; his strongly constitutional and parliamentary instincts were all for accepting the Montagu–Chelmsford Reforms. He was secular minded and elitist and was appalled at the kind of demagogic religious politics that the Khilafat movement brought in its train. At the Nagpur Congress of 1920 he denounced Gandhi's programme and was driven to the margins. He tried to give some shape to Muslim politics after the collapse of the Khilafat movement and he continued to seek an alliance with Congress. With the rejection of separate electorates by Congress at an all-parties conference in Calcutta in 1928 Jinnah gave up in despair and in 1929 went into self-imposed exile in Britain. The Western-educated Muslims were, however, to call him back to lead the Indian Muslims in the new political dispensation of the 1930s. He returned in 1935, but it was a different Jinnah, no longer reluctant to play the communal card. He had not yet rejected the possibility of working with Congress but his rhetoric now was to brand it as a Hindu communal organization, merely the other side of the coin to the Hindu Mahasabha. Ironically, with the political structures of the very Khilafat movement he had despised, he found the machinery for rebuilding the Muslim League as an all-India party in response to both the Communal Award provisions of 1932, confirming Muslim separate electorates (see below), and the Government of India Act of 1935.

One recourse for Congress in meeting the charge of its being a Hindu communal body was to highlight the role of Muslims within the party. There were major recruits from the Khilafat movement, both from the Westernized elites, e.g. Dr Ansari, alumni of Aligarh, a doctor in Delhi, and from the ulamas. Azad had always been the most convinced supporter of satyagraha amongst the priests and he became an outstanding recruit to Congress. There was a hint of tokenism about his high status in the party, but he was a man of exceptional talent, and was to be a close colleague of Nehru in later years. (It is worth reading his autobiography, *India Wins Freedom*, 1959.) A rather surprising recruit to the policies of non-violence was the Pathan leader Abdul Ghaffar Khan, bringing his 'Red Shirts' movement in the North West Frontier Province into alliance with the Congress. In the 1930s Congress forbade any member to be likewise a member of the Hindu Mahasabha. But such measures could not conceal the fact that Gandhi had largely failed in his endeavour to win the loyalties of the Indian Muslims.

If Gandhi's bid to rally the Muslims ultimately failed, can we say he had any greater success in winning the support of the untouchables? To approach that question one has first to ask what attitudes Gandhi adopted towards the caste system. This is to open a Pandora's box, so extensive is the literature on caste. Cohn's study (1971) is an excellent introduction, Basham's (1954) is valuable for its historical setting and Lannoy's (1971) for its more contemporary account. David Mandelbaum's two-volume study (1970) provides a more detailed follow-up.

An elementary error is to confuse the varna system with caste, although the confusion is easy enough to understand. The varna system comprised the three twice-born castes – brahmins or priests, kshatriyas or warriors and vaisha or merchants – and the sudras or peasants. Outside the varna system lay the outcastes or untouchables. The three twice-born castes were entitled to wear the sacred thread, a symbol of their initiation (hence being born again) into the Hindu religion, acquiring a special mantra etc. Whether the varnas are seen as classes or estates they are quite different from the jati, the real caste group, a much more specific localized community, ascriptive (determined by birth) and generally occupational. Within the jati there would be a smaller exogamous group, known as biradari, the local caste group. It has been calculated that in any one linguistic area there might be 50–200 castes with as many as 500–2,000 subcastes.

Gandhi's views on the varna system were relatively unambiguous. He retained a belief in caste as defining function – varnashram. All four varnas would reinforce one another: the wisdom of the brahmins; the fighting spirit of the kshatriya; the business acumen of the vaisha; the spirit of service of the sudra. He himself came from the modh bania caste, a grocer's caste. In the scrupulous accounting he kept of the funds of the constructive movement he prided himself on his good vaisha habits. In Kathiawad, the merchant vaisha castes, through their absorption of Jainism, had thrown off traditional deference to brahmins. Gandhi himself was not inhibited in challenging their Sanatinist Hindu orthodoxy. Adopting the role of sanyassin was another traditional mode of escaping brahminical constraints. But his theory of varnashram fell short of the radicalism of the Arya Samaj movement: Dayanand had rejected the ascriptive view of caste and insisted that only under inspection would each individual discover to which varna he belonged. It was this idea of varna as based on achievement which made the Arya Samaj so popular a movement. Gandhi's radicalism took a different form. He believed that the twice-born castes should share in the sudra ideal of service, and that all caste Hindus should devote themselves to alleviating the suffering of the untouchables. His ideal was to reabsorb the untouchables within the sudra caste.

None of this necessarily sheds any light on Gandhi's views on caste as jati. His idealization of the village would suggest that he retained a sympathy for the jajmani system of social inter-dependence. His controversial education system at Wardha seemed to emphasize the need to transmit craft or occupational skills on a hereditary basis. One way round this tendency to see socially reactionary elements in Gandhi's thinking is to utilize the concept of the traditionalist as modernizer; Gandhi wanted to revitalize the virtues, as he saw them, of the village community.

Anti-untouchability did not initially predominate in the con-structive movement – khadi was the major platform in the 1920s – but already a number of relevant reforms were pursued. Gandhi's ambition was to reintegrate the untouchables within the social and cultural life of caste–Hindu society: for example, the untouchables were to be given access to public facilities, above all to wells. They were to be allowed to worship in temples: there was, for example, a major satyagraha campaign to open the Vykom temple to untouchables in Travancore, in Southern India, where anti-untouchability had been taken to extreme lengths. Here it was even polluting for the shadow of an untouch-able to fall on a brahmin, and untouchables had to ring a bell to warn brahmins of their approach. Prohibition work was linked to these campaigns, for drunkenness was seen as particularly rampant amongst untouchables and it was felt that the ending of such conduct would facilitate their social acceptability. (It was also, of course, a way of embarrassing a government still dependent on its excise revenue.) The Arya Samaj, however, felt it was making a far more radical effort to reach the untouchables. Shraddhanand resigned from Congress in 1922 in protest at the ineffectuality of the Congress reform programme and it was not until Gandhi's struggle with Dr Ambedkar, the leader of India's untouchables, that anti-untouchability became a central issue in the constructive movement.

The confrontation came over the Communal Award of 14 August 1932, a measure by which Prime Minister Ramsay Macdonald imagined he had pleased both Dr Ambedkar, by granting a separate electorate for the untouchables for an exper-imental period of 20 years, and Gandhi, by allowing the untouch-ables a chance to vote again in general seats. The niceties of constitutional arrangements, however, were not Gandhi's main concern: he saw here merely an attempt to divide the untouchables from caste–Hindu society and the destruction of his passionately held vision of a reintegrated society. On 20 September Gandhi, then detained in Yeravda gaol, began a fast to the death against the Communal Award, the 'epic fast' as it came to be known, and the most extreme use to which he put the fast in satyagraha.

Dr Ambedkar had emerged by 1932 as the all-India leader of the untouchables and in that capacity had attended the Round Table Conferences in London. Here was a classic example of Raj and Congress seeking the loyalty of the same community. Born in 1891, the fourteenth child of a major in the Indian Army, headmaster of a military school. He belonged to the Maharastrian mahar untouchable caste. He was to emerge as India's greatest constitutional lawyer and did most to draft the Indian Constitution of 1950. A distinguished career in education and the law and a period serving in the progressive administration of the princely state of Baroda (one in which his untouchable status had led to endless humiliation) had brought him to prominence by 1918: the Southborough Commission on franchise had interviewed him in preparation for the Montagu–Chelmsford Reforms. Ambedkar's was a revolt against the dependency status of Indian untouchables; he rejected caste–Hindu Congress organizations in favour of the untouchables' own. His themes were self-help, self-elevation, self-respect. He was aware of the political significance of so large a minority and of its vital role in India's democratic future. Initially he favoured joint electorates, with reserved seats, believing that in a system of universal suffrage their numbers would guarantee substantial representation. His biographer (Dhananjay Keer, 1971) claims that it was Gandhi's opposition even to reserved seats at the Second Round Table Conference of 1931 which led him to change his mind and go for a separate electorate. This marked the beginnings of a 'bitter and life-long enmity' between Gandhi and Ambedkar (Lynch, 1969, p. 132). He saw Gandhi simply as the leader of caste–Hindus who had grotesquely exploited his people; a man he distrusted and came to hate. (Not all untouchable leaders felt the same, however: the Madras leader, M. C. Rajah, had agreed to joint electorates at a conference in February 1932.)

Eventually Gandhi's fast, which many saw as moral blackmail, prevailed and on 25 September the Poona Pact was signed. There would be primary elections, in which the untouchables would elect three candidates for each reserved seat; these would then be voted for by the general franchise. The *quid pro quo* for Ambedkar was a greatly increased number of reserved seats in the legislatures from that initially allocated in the Communal Award: an increase of, for example, from 71 to 149 in the central legislative assembly.

It was after this pact that Gandhi decided to devote an entire year to the anti-untouchability campaign. He set up a Harijan Sevak Sangh (Order for the Service of Harijans), founded a new weekly, *Harijan*, and set out from his new base at Wardha on 7 November on an extensive campaign tour which lasted until June of the following year. It took physical courage to challenge entrenched prejudice: in June 1933 a bomb intended for Gandhi landed on another vehicle, injuring seven. But once again the constructive programme had taken Gandhi away from the campaign of civil disobedience; and when he expressed the obscurantist view that an earthquake in Bihar in January 1934 was divine judgement on untouchability, doubts were raised amongst Congress leaders as to his suitability as their leader. In October 1934 Gandhi resigned from the Congress Party.

This chapter has pointed out the limitations of Gandhi's power. Through the constructive movement Gandhi had sought the loyalty of the Indian Muslims and the untouchables, both to create a revitalized homogeneous society, above all at village level, and to further the cause of integral nationalism. But for all the extraordinary powers of satyagraha and the fast, there were limits to his power and his appeal. To most Muslims he still appeared a Hindu; to many untouchables, a caste Hindu. The two great religious communities were beginning terrifyingly to drift apart. 'Casteism' did not represent the same threat of separatism, except with the non-brahmin Dravidian movement in the south, but Gandhi had antagonized the untouchable leader Dr Ambedkar, who saw mere duplicity in the Poona Pact and sought an independent line for his community. He was not impressed by the Gandhian social uplift programme: he believed that in economic advance lay the best way forward for the untouchables. Both the Indian Muslims and the untouchables saw in the Raj an alternative patron to Gandhi and Congress. Old, lonely, puzzled and, perhaps in a way he himself could not fathom, increasingly angry, Gandhi sought a new occasion to throw off the Raj and yet realize his vision of the Kingdom of Righteousness, Ram Rajha.

6 'Quit India'

Gandhi's remaining years were played out against a background of war and communal violence. He was to know loneliness, despair and doubt, as he seemed to have failed in all his endeavours. Yet his radicalism deepened in old age and he displayed a continuing resilience in the pursuit of political freedom and social transformation. Even if the Raj's intentions remained ambiguous towards Indians, even towards itself, it was clear that India herself had entered a period of transition, and this let loose a murderous war of succession.

Something similar had occurred with the collapse of East India Company rule in 1857 and events between 1935 and 1947, in terms of their violence and popular insurrection, find their only parallel in the colonial period with the upheavals of the Great Rebellion. The war-time threat to India from Japan now put entirely new pressures on the validity of Gandhi's strategy of non-violence. His own response was to emphasize even more strongly the necessity for British withdrawal: in freedom, Indians would themselves work out the solution to self-defence and problems of Hindu–Muslim rivalry. With his resignation from Congress in 1934, Gandhi's political status had become highly anomalous and his ingenuity was put even more to the test as he tried to press his solutions to events on his Congress colleagues. Some historians see Gandhi at the height of his powers during the salt satyagraha, but a strong case can be made for seeing his most supreme effort in the Quit India movement of 1942 and his anguished stand against communalism, in Noakhali and Calcutta, in the last years of his life.

Constitutional Manœuvres

In the aftermath of the civil disobedience campaign of 1930–4 the Raj sought once again to regain the moral initiative through the constitutional changes it tried to introduce with the Government of India Act of 1935. In retrospect, given that many of its measures provided a political framework for the successor states of India and Pakistan, the immense amount of time put into devising it might seem justified, but at the time it appeared, to quote Judith Brown (1985, p. 274) 'a battered and ill-liked package of partial reforms'. It failed in its quest to fashion a federal government at the centre; its extension of provincial autonomy provided invaluable experience for the sub-continent's political elite, but in the short run it served only further to exacerbate Hindu–Muslim rivalry. Gandhi gave both the provincial and the federal aspects of the new Act an initial measure of support: later he was to display hostility, bordering on disgust.

The fate of the federal plan of government lay in the hands of the Indian princes. Although they rarely spoke with one voice, it began to get through to them that they must make some moves in their own self-interest, and the authorities in London were quick to pounce on their expression of support at the first Round Table Conference of 1930 for some federal solution to the future relationship between princely and British India. Conservative die-hard opposition to any devolution of power at the centre would be diminished if the princes, traditional allies of the Raj, were granted some constraining role in a more self-governing central administration, and indeed the princes were offered remarkably generous terms. In the new bicameral federal legislature proposed in the Act, the princes would nominate one-third of the seats in the legislative assembly and two-fifths in the upper house or council of state; the federation would be delayed until half the number of princely states entitled to sit in the council of state had acceded. With such conservative princely backing, the Raj was ready to introduce diarchy at the centre: the Governor-General in council would hold on to the portfolios of defence and external affairs but the remainder would be held by ministers responsible to the legislature. The new Viceroy, Lord Linlithgow, successor to Willingdon in 1936, made very considerable efforts to persuade the princes to accede: he believed that the implementation of the federal measures of the Act had to keep pace with the provincial reforms if the overall scheme was to work.

To Congress radicals, the whole federal scheme was appalling. For Nehru, the only possible political future for India lay through the decision-making of a democratically elected constituent assembly; this attempt to foist the influence of reactionary feudal states on a future constitution for India was intolerable. Gandhi's initial concern was more with the reserved portfolios, but he likewise became alarmed at the princely states' incorporation in a new Indian constitution before any substantial progress had been achieved in political and social reform. The conventional line for Congress was to accept a federal scheme for British India but delay membership for the states.

Gandhi became actively involved in the debate through his seemingly perverse handling of a dispute between Congress and the Thakore of Rajkot, the family state of the Gandhis. It was a complex dispute in which the Thakore had reneged on the composition of a committee of reform he had agreed to set up in response to a satyagraha. Gandhi took up the struggle and embarked on a fast on 3 March 1939. He appealed to Viceroy Linlithgow and the Chief Justice of India ruled in his favour, only for him to discover that his own men could be included on the committee only at the expense of representatives of the landlords and Muslims of Rajkot to whom he had likewise promised places. In some embarrassment, Gandhi called off the fast. Maybe the Rajkot fast had only ever been a smokescreen for his political showdown with Subhas Bose, but it did suggest that Gandhi was losing his touch.

With the outbreak of war the prospect of federation had to be shelved, although the princes had in any case declared at a meeting in Bombay in June 1939 that they found the scheme unacceptable, even though Linlithgow had succeeded in rallying support from some two-fifths of the states. (See John Glendevon's sympathetic account of his father's viceroyalty, *The Viceroy at Bay*, 1971.) It was to be left to Vallabhai Patel, as Home Minister after independence, to organize the integration of the great majority of the princely states into the new state of India, leaving behind in the process a still unresolved dispute between the two successor states over Kashmir.

In the meantime the Raj experienced greater success, if not entirely in ways it sought, with the provincial measures of the new Act. The franchise was extended to some 30 million people – about one-sixth of those who would have been enfranchised under universal suffrage – and the system of diarchy gave way to full provincial autonomy. Such liberalization, of course, reflected the Raj's pursuit of new collaborators in the administration of empire, but it constituted an offer of power which Congress provincial politicians found impossible to resist. It was yet another stage in the old Congress debate between holding on to a long term vision of full independence or capitalizing on the short term gains which such constitutional advances offered. For the radicals, such limited gains were seen to be treacherous distractions from the freedom struggle, and Nehru, president of the Congress in 1936, stood out against Congress ambitions for forming provincial governments. Gandhi had to exercise all his skills as arbiter. The specific issue disputed was the reserve powers of the provincial governors under section 93 of the Act, which seemingly cancelled out the liberal concessions. In the end, Gandhi swayed Congress into entering office on these terms, having obtained vague promises from the Raj that the powers would be used sparingly.

Gandhi had already given his blessing to a return to parliamentary politics with the revival of the Swaraj Party for the 1934 elections to the central legislative assembly. In 1937, Congress did exceptionally well in the provincial elections, winning 716 out of 1,585 seats and forming Congress ministries in Madras, Bihar, Orissa, Central Provinces and United Provinces. Space does not permit any detailed examination of the Congress ministries, but significant moves were made to question the power of the zamindars and to relieve the conditions of the richer peasants. Congress ministers also took up some aspects of the constructive movement, most enthusiastically, prohibition. But Gandhi's natural aversion to power politics began to surface and he felt increasingly disgusted by the way Congress politicians exercised their new found powers of patronage. The decision by Linlithgow on 17 October 1939 to declare India at war with Germany without any attempt to consult the Congress ministries provided Gandhi with a pretext for insisting that the ministries resign, which they did on 19 October 1939. In fact, Congress had run into many problems, and for all the seeming recklessness in throwing away political power at this juncture, it may have been a necessary move in order to set its own house in order and regain its moral authority.

Much the most disturbing legacy of the Congress ministries of 1937–9 was the worsening relationship between Hindus and Muslims. This was in part a consequence of Congress errors, in part the unscrupulous exploitation of such errors by a now self-consciously communal Muslim League led by Jinnah. An underlying Muslim fear of such progressive experimentation in constitutional and democratic forms was that majority rule would lead to Hindu Raj. Fatally, the Congress ministries, if often in only minor provocative ways, were to feed this fear. The singing of the Congress 'anthem' – the Bande Mataram (Hail Mother-land), Bankim Chandra Chatterjee's poem from a novel exhort-ing Hindu patriotism against Muslim rule – is one example (although one of the premiers, Rajagopalachari, was to dis-courage the party from singing it in the Madras provincial legislature). In many ways, this 'Hindu' content to the Congress programme derived from Gandhi's use of religious symbolism; his own commitment to the Wardha educational scheme with its seeming Hindu caste dimension, was a further cause of antag-onism. His championing of Hindi, seemingly at the expense of Urdu, was far more threatening.

Congress had gained only some five per cent of the Muslim seats in the 1937 provincial elections. The Muslim League had not done very much better, winning only 22.6 per cent. In the Muslim majority provinces of Bengal and the Punjab there were Muslim but not League ministries, with Muslims sharing power with Hindus and Sikhs in the Unionist ministry under Sikander Hyat Khan in the Punjab. Such Muslim League weakness, however, hardly excused Nehru's blindness to its sensibilities when he insisted that any Muslim representative in the UP ministry would have to take an oath of loyalty to Congress. Jinnah was quick to capitalize on such insensitivity. Congress, he argued, had emerged in its true colours as fascist dictators. The Muslims would always be victims as a minority in Hindu-dominated parliamentary politics. He declared the occasion of the Congress ministries' resignations a day of deliverance for Muslims. He switched his tactics from seeking protection for Muslims as a minority within a federal constitution to declaring that the Muslim minority was, in fact, a national majority. The Muslim League was beginning to attract support in Muslim minority areas, above all in the UP. When Jinnah declared at the Lahore Congress of 1940 that the aim of the Muslim League was the independent state of Pakistan, it was everyone's guess whether he was using this as a bargaining counter or it had indeed become his primary objective. Together with the outbreak of war, Indian politics were taking on a new air of menace.

Gandhi's Dilemma: Collaboration or Resistance

The least researched of Gandhi's civil disobedience movements, the 'Quit India' rebellion of August 1942, may yet emerge as the one that best reveals the truly radical, if still ambiguous, content of his political values. It will not do to play down the rebellion as 'unGandhian'. One has to stress once again Gandhi's capacity for evolution. It is vital to build up a clear understanding of his intent in August 1942; this may lend a more contemporary relevance to his ideas and allow connections between Gandhian values and today's liberation struggles in South Africa and against neo-colonialism, as well as the continuing struggle for justice within the Indian sub-continent.

Gandhi found himself caught up in a highly complex set of competing strategies. How was India to defend itself against Japanese aggression at a time of a resurgent authoritarian Raj? Gandhi had to juggle with numerous alternatives: collaboration between Congress and the Raj to meet the war-time emergency, a view vigorously put forward by Rajagopalachari and viewed sympathetically by Nehru; a wholly different view of seeing in the Axis powers the instrument for India's liberation from imperialism, a line of action pursued by Subhas Bose (see below); or a popular revolutionary movement from below, favoured by the leftist elements in Congress, above all by Jayaprakash Narayan of the Congress Socialists, and by underground terrorist groups. The question of national self-defence was inextricably linked to the threat to national integrity posed by Muslim separatism. Gandhi's answer, if highly idiosyncratic and eclectic, bore most resemblance to popular revolution.

Evaluation of Gandhi's response to the war-time crisis depends in part on assessing the role of India in Japan's own war plans. India was, in fact, peripheral. Economic and strategic factors led to Japanese expansion into South-East Asia: Malaya would provide rubber and tea, the East Indies oil, bauxite and rubber. Concern to close off supplies along the Burma road to China, Japan's greatest territorial sphere of interest, led to the conquest of Burma, but Japan saw no advantage in 1942 in pressing on with any attempted invasion of India. On the other hand, Japan saw herself as the liberator of Asian peoples from oppressive European colonialism and here Japan's presence posed a threat to British rule and offered a potential ally to the Congress Party. It was not to be until late 1944, however, that Japan saw advantage in invading India as a means of restoring her by then badly damaged morale. Allied victory in the Imphal–Kohima sector was to be a critical turning point in the war, the successes of 1944–5 reversing the defeats of 1941–2, and by January 1945 the land route to China was open once again. Perhaps India was at no great risk from Japan at the time Gandhi launched the Quit India campaign, though he might be excused for exaggerating the danger of invasion by Japan and acting on the desperate need for Indians to set their own house in order before confronting this new threat of conquest. On the other hand, if Gandhi was not so concerned with the prospect of Japanese invasion, and his actions suggest that he was not, then this might endorse the view that his essential aim remained the liberation of India from British imperialism.

If the federal proposals of the Act of 1935 should be construed as essentially a holding operation rather than a statement of intent on the dismantling of empire, the conduct of the Raj during the early years of the war suggests an even more committed view of the continuing role of empire. In some ways this was merely a prising apart of positions always held in uneasy alliance, a metropolitan one, less emotionally involved in empire and more susceptible to dialogue, and that of the Raj itself, more keenly aware of its status and of the struggle for power within the sub-continent. There is a strong case to be made that in the context of the war-time emergency the Raj lost its head and sought a showdown with Congress. With the resignation of the Congress ministries many provinces went over to the Advisory system, really rule by the Governor working through British and Indian officials, (in today's parlance, President's rule); and arguably the writ of the Raj never ran as unchecked as during the war. There were even contingency plans to deport Gandhi to East Africa (Aden), anticipating by over a decade a similar exile for the EOKA nationalist Cypriot leader Archbishop Makarios (though in his case to the Seychelles). In fact, when the crisis came in 1942, Raj officialdom acted under existing war-time emergency legislation and did not even resort to martial law, even if it was quick to introduce indemnity legislation to cover those officials who had overstepped permitted limits. It was hardly a climate, however, in which Congress was likely to establish a closer working relationship with government.

With the mission of Sir Stafford Cripps, a member of the War Cabinet and Lord Privy Seal in 1942, the metropolitan government introduced a more flexible approach. There was much here which was mere window-dressing, a front to persuade the USA that Britain shared its anti-colonialist rhetoric and perhaps simply a device for winning goodwill from the Raj's traditional allies in the sub-continent, the princes, landowners and Indian administrators. There is considerable evidence to show that both the Secretary of State for India, Leo Amery, and Prime Minister Winston Churchill shared many of Viceroy Linlithgow's assumptions on the need to shore up imperial power. But there is evidence also that Cripps himself was sincere, even if he was never in a position to fulfil the promises made. There was, however, enough in his package to force Congress into a dialogue.

Cripps believed he was in a position to offer Congress a quasi-cabinet system at the centre on the same model as that which had operated successfully at the provincial level, with the same proviso that the Viceroy sparingly exercised his legal right to intervene. The sticking point was whether or not cabinet responsibility would also include the portfolio of defence, formerly excluded under the diarchic structure of 1935, and here Whitehall, the Viceroy and General and Wavell as Commander-in-Chief of the Indian Army would not budge; it seemed inconceivable that responsibility for war-time strategy should be handed over to a Congress minister. The south had been the first to experience Japanese aggression. Vizagapatam was bombed on 6 April 1942 and coastal cities, including the Madras administration, were evacuated. It was this danger which spurred the southerner Rajagopalachari to press Congress to accept the Cripps offer, although Rajagopalachari was a politician whose spell in office between 1937 and 1939 had convinced him that future Congress rulers of an independent India could only profit from all such experience. Nehru, if with greater reluctance and for different reasons, was also tempted: he sought an outcome in which Congress could harness its energies to a struggle against fascism. Gandhi's approach was his customary one when out of sympathy with his colleagues: he distanced himself from events and allowed the Congress high command to sort out the situation as best it might. The Cripps mission eventually broke down on the issue of the defence portfolio, but it is also clear that the licence the proposals offered for any province to withdraw from a post-war federal India played on deepening Congress anxieties about Muslim separatism and the future of princely India.

Congress was offered a totally different way out of its dilemma over war-time strategy – that of collaboration with Japan – by yet another twist in the lurid career of Subhas Bose. It is doubtful whether this was ever a serious alternative, though it is worth speculating how differently Congress might have responded had Subhas Bose made more significant advances in organizing an Indian National Army in exile by the time of the critical months of the summer of 1942. It is also a story that raises the issue of Gandhi's own problematic relationship with Bose and it is worth digressing to examine it in some detail.

Subhas Chandra Bose, born in 1897, a Bengali whose radical nationalism owed much to that tradition of Bengali patriotism so fiercely revealed in response to the partition of Bengal in 1905, was always on the extremist wing of the Indian National Congress, though, as is the way with extremists, it became difficult to say whether this made him a man of the Right or of the Left. One view of Bose is to stress his highly ambivalent attitude towards authority; his need both to be accepted by the establishment and to reject it. Symptomatic of this was his success in the ICS examination in 1920, followed almost immediately by his resignation in May 1921 in order to join the freedom struggle. Such ambivalence certainly coloured his relationship with Gandhi, whose respect he always sought yet with whom he was to be in frequent conflict. They first met in July 1921, in Bombay, on Bose's return to India from England. Gandhi failed to impress him as a leader: he wrote, 'my reason told me clearly, again and again, that there was a deplorable lack of clarity in the plan which the Mahatma had formulated and that he himself did not have a clear idea of the successive stages of the campaign which would bring India to her cherished goal of freedom' (1948, p. 82). Where Gandhi failed as a political guru for Bose, C. R. Das, the Bengal Congress leader, succeeded, and it was he who became an alternative father figure for Bose until his premature death in 1925. Bose in may ways then took up Das's struggle to defend the interests of Bengal within the Congress, and central to Bose's relationship with Gandhi and with Congress was outraged Bengali pride at the usurpation of Bengal's dominant role by upstart provinces such as Gujarat. But Bose was also heir to the tradition of revolutionary violence in Bengal, and it was this radicalism which gave rise to the friction with Gandhi.

Whereas Gandhi successfully bridged the generation gap between himself and the young Nehru, he failed to do so with Bose. Bose was both diffident and highly ambitious and resented the way in which the young Nehru was always one step ahead of him. His status within Congress was not advanced by a long spell in Europe in the early 1930s, during which he came under the sway of European authoritarian movements. He claimed to stand for some synthesis of communism and fascism, attracted both by the ruthless use of state power by Stalin in building up the economy and by the military discipline of fascism.

Gandhi's tactic was to try to contain Bose by giving him responsibility, and he succeeded Nehru as Congress president in 1938. He now characteristically rebelled against Gandhi's leadership and insisted on a right to stand for a second term as president by election in 1939: in this he was, in fact, to succeed, but this challenged the assumed right of the Congress high command to nominate the presidency. It was at this stage that Gandhi brought about a mass resignation of the working committee, forcing Bose's resignation and driving him into setting up a rival organization, the Forward Block. Gandhi, if still respected, was now branded as leader of an older generation of reformist leaders allied to the interests of Indian capitalists. Bose raised the possibility of an immediate return to civil disobedience. Always under police surveillance because of his suspected links with terrorists, he was arrested. On his release he decided to escape the country, and after a journey which laid the foundations of his legend, Bose arrived in Berlin on 2 April 1941.

Gandhi was clearly excited by Bose's adventure and listened to his radio broadcasts from Germany. It was the view of Maulana Azad that by December 1941 Gandhi's outlook on the war had changed: 'his admiration for Subhas Bose unconsciously coloured his view about the whole war situation' (1959, p. 36). When Gandhi heard a rumour of Bose's death in a plane crash in April 1942 he wrote to his mother, 'The whole nation mourns with you the death of your brave son. I share your sorrow to the full' (Mihir Bose 1982, p. 197).

Bose's strategy was in part founded on the Nazi–Soviet pact – it made sense of his own attempts to fuse the two totalitarian ideologies – but that had already begun to fall apart with the German invasion of Russia in June 1941. Bose made little headway with his attempt to build up an Indian army in Europe from Indian prisoners of war (in the end, some 4,000 out of 12,000 were to join the Indian Legion) and similar recruitment from Japanese prisoners of war in Malaya, under the leadership of Mohan Singh, made equally little progress. It was therefore towards the East that Bose began to turn, sensing a lack of support from Hitler, if somewhat greater interest from Mussolini.

But he did not set sail for Japan until 8 February 1943, and only took up the task of organizing the Indian National Army after his arrival in Singapore on 12 July 1943, long after Gandhi had launched the desperate gamble of the Quit India movement.

The striking successes of Japan, with the fall of Singapore in November 1941, the conquest of Burma and the threat to Assam at Imphal by May 1942, may well have convinced Gandhi that the British Empire was on the brink of collapse. Even more alarming was evidence of widespread defeatism among the population of those areas of Eastern India at risk. Assam, Bengal, even India itself, seemed on the verge of chaos. Might Gandhi have positively sought out the Japanese in the spirit of France's Pétain if Subhas Bose had made greater headway with his government-in-exile? Certainly Gandhi became convinced there would be no cause for quarrel between India and Japan were India no longer part of the British Empire, and the Japanese had not included India in their Greater East Asia Co-Prosperity scheme. But it hardly makes sense to suppose that Gandhi would have warmed either to Bose, a rebel to Congress authority, or to the militaristic imperialist government of the Japanese General Tojo. In the event, Gandhi's solution was to be more in the spirit of the French Resistance than of Pétainism.

A countervailing influence to Subhas Bose's authoritarian socialism came from Jayaprakash Narayan's Democratic Socialism, although he did not formally commit himself to such principles until 1946. Narayan's relationships with Gandhi and Nehru were strikingly different from Bose's. He had likewise joined the freedom struggle in 1921 and while making up at American universities for lost educational opportunities in India his young wife stayed at the Sabarmati ashram. Gandhi befriended Narayan on his return to India in 1929 and he and Nehru became intimates. Nehru gave his blessing to Narayan's Congress Socialist Party, set up in 1934, appointing Narayan to his working committee in 1936. It is open to question whether Gandhi did more to lead Narayan away from his Marxism, or whether the latter led Gandhi towards his own more radical vision of the liberation struggle. Certainly Narayan began to question the Soviet Union's commitment to centralization and to large-scale collectivization in favour of a more democratic, decentralized, village-orientated programme, though he did not share Gandhi's aversion to machinery and was already visualizing his own agro-industrial solution towards village development. His solution to the war-time crisis lay in out-and-out non-cooperation, if necessary with recourse to violence. It was here that he and Subhas Bose shared a temperamental inclination to the violent overthrow of empire. Narayan was arrested on 7 March 1940, and remained in gaol until his escape on 8 November 1942, but in letters smuggled out by his wife he advocated an armed underground uprising against the Raj. These were published by the government in October 1941, in an effort to discredit Congress. Gandhi's initial response was to question the appropriateness of a violent struggle while a non-violent strategy was on trial, but the evidence suggests he was drawing closer to Narayan's position.

Rebellion

If satyagraha tactics could provide no solution for India's defence against aggression then Gandhi would be forced to recognize that his political beliefs were insubstantial. But there was no question of simply handing India over to the Japanese; it was a question of how most effectively to meet Japanese aggression. As with all Gandhi's major decisions, he moved only gradually towards an answer. He welcomed the resignation of the Congress ministries in October 1939, but by July 1940 Rajagopalachari had persuaded Congress to offer to collaborate with the government again on the condition that a provisional national – which meant Congress – government was set up immediately. Gandhi was relieved that nothing came from such approaches and as a counter-move encouraged a return to limited civil disobedience in the form of individual satyagraha. Some 23,000 followers were arrested in 1940–1 but with no solution in sight, the Congress high command approached Gandhi in January 1942 to take up the leadership once again. Gandhi's response came in a letter taken by Mira Behn to the working committee at Allahabad in April. This was the 'Quit India' resolution, which the Congress working committee was formally to approve in early July and whose confirmation by the All-India Congress Commitee (AICC) in Bombay on 7 August was to launch the most violent assault on British rule in India since 1857. Their resolution reads in part:

> The AICC, therefore, repeats with all emphasis the demand for the withdrawal of the British power from India. On the

89

declaration of India's independence, a provisional Government will be formed and free India will become an ally of the United Nations, sharing with them in the trials and tribulations of the joint enterprise of the struggle for freedom. The provisional Government can only be formed by the co-operation of the principal parties and groups in the country. It will thus be a composite Government, representative of all important sections of the people of India. Its primary functions must be to defend India and resist aggression with all the armed as well as the non-violent forces at its command, together with its Allied Powers, and to promote the well-being and progress of the workers in the fields and factories and elsewhere to whom essentially all power and authority must belong. . . . Freedom will enable India to resist aggression effectively with the people's united will and strength behind it . . .

The AICC would yet again, at this last moment, in the interest of world freedom, renew this appeal to Britain and the United Nations. But the Committee feels that it is no longer justified in holding the nation back from endeavouring to assert its will against an imperialist and authoritarian Government which dominates over it and prevents it from functioning in its own interest and in the interest of humanity. The Committee resolves, therefore, to sanction, for the vindication of India's inalienable right to freedom and independence, the starting of a mass struggle on non-violent lines on the widest possible scale, so that the country might utilize all the non-violent strength it has gathered during the last 22 years of peaceful struggle. Such a struggle must inevitably be under the leadership of Gandhiji and the Committee requests him to take the lead and guide the nation in the steps to be taken . . . (Philips, 1962, p. 342).

The decision to adopt the Quit India resolution remains highly controversial and Gandhi's own expectations of the outcome are still in contention. In his own mind he had not ruled out some kind of deal with the British: if the British would grant India freedom, he felt it perfectly feasible that a new Indian government might decide to offer Britain its help in the fight against the Axis powers. But if Gandhi entertained any real belief that the Raj would accept such a deal, then his political naiveté at a time of national crisis is, of course, cruelly exposed. There is evidence that Gandhi supposed Linlithgow might restart negotiations after the resolution had been passed. Francis Hutchins, on the other hand, in the only full-scale study to date of the Quit India movement (1973), sees a different imperative in Gandhi's strategy. He believes Gandhi had finally nerved himself for that mass movement against the Raj which would not only throw off foreign rule but drive India forwards to the social revolution he sought, the very breakdown of government forcing India back into self-reliance on its 700,000 villages. Gandhi believed the masses were now ready for such a non-violent struggle, but, if the protest should spill over into violence, then, providing this was spontaneous and in self-defence, it would be condoned. Hutchins' argument seems unable to establish anything more positive than Gandhi's condoning violence: his preference remained for non-violence. But this time no 'Chauri Chaura' would create a pretext for calling off the uprising, and Indians would thus find themselves in a strong position to meet Japanese aggression by offering some form of non-violent non-cooperation. Indians could not be accused of cowardice.

This is not the place for a detailed description of the events of the initial August uprising. Even so, there was evidence of a widespread rebellion in Northern India; rail and telegraph communications between Calcutta and Delhi had been systematically vandalized.

Swift reprisals by government against the Congress high command and the AICC immediately robbed the movement of its major leaders and the possibility of any centralized control; it is this fact alone which has led historians to characterize the rising as 'spontaneous'. Second-tier leadership had to take over and the rebellion had to be organized at the local level. In large areas of Bihar and the Eastern UP the rebellion was devastating; Bombay was another centre of revolt. It could be argued that such rebellion owed little to Gandhi and the Congress high command and derived from quite separate local factors. It is certainly the case that Bihar and the Eastern UP had been radicalized under the influence of the Congress Socialists, and this could be interpreted as another example of an 'autonomous' peasant movement. Stephen Henningham has explained its ultimate failure in terms of that characteristic split between rich and poor peasant protest (Guha, II, 1983). Even so, legitimate claims can be made for seeing this as the largest-scale peasant uprising against colonial rule since 1857. These were also areas where many migrant estate workers had returned from South-East Asia, bringing tales of the collapse of British rule and of British betrayal, spreading defeatism and anti-British feeling among the local population. Ironically, it was the large-scale presence of troops in these areas, assembled for the defence of the north-east frontier, which made possible the relatively quick suppression of the initial August uprising. Subsequently the political underground, led in large part by Narayan and supported by pro-Bose elements, sustained guerrilla warfare against the government into the autumn of 1943. Hutchins claims that the Quit India uprising was a success in that it led the Raj to revise its assumptions. Linlithgow and Amery now thought in terms of a retreat from empire. The stage had been set for the transfer of power.

Gandhi had been arrested early on 9 August 1942 and taken to detention at the Aga Khan's summer palace in Poona. It was to be a prolonged and often sad period of imprisonment, with the deaths of Mahadev Desai and of Gandhi's wife, Kasturbai. On 10 February 1943 he undertook his only fast directed against a Viceroy; this was in protest at Linlithgow's attempt to saddle him with responsibility for the outbreak of violence in August 1942. Gandhi's counter-argument was that if the government had not locked up the Congress leadership, the protest would have been directed along non-violent lines. This seems to suggest that Gandhi still rejected the role of violence and certainly at the time Gandhians sought a return to the constructive programme and the abandonment of the guerrilla movement. This may, however, simply be a rejection of *pre-meditated* violence and leaves open the possibility that Gandhi did not reject its spontaneous expression.

The Last Years: Communalism and Partition

Serious illness led to Gandhi's release on 6 May 1944. He now had to pick up the pieces in a political India very different from that of August 1942. Gandhi never experienced such isolation as during the last years of his life. In all the major spheres of his activity he felt himself in conflict with the evolution of events. Gandhi stood against the tide, yet he could never bring himself openly to rebel against the decisions taken by the Congress high command. He maintained this personal democratic approach until the end.

In terms of power politics, these were years of the colonial end-game, dominated by two increasingly enmeshed policies – the granting of freedom and the partition of the sub-continent. Against this background of political intrigue, Indian society was drifting towards appalling communal violence in which it is calculated that some 250,000 people lost their lives and over two million turned migrant to one or other of the successor states of India and Pakistan. Gandhi drew on all his spiritual reserves to try to stem these developments, although at the time of his release he was ill with amoebic dysentery and, at 75 years of age, he was making almost impossible demands on himself. In these years of crisis he had also to revise his estimate of the constructive programme and seek new ways to realize his dream of Ram Rajha. This account will largely follow the scholarship of Pyarelal (1956) and the personal recollections of N. K. Bose (1953), the two men possibly closest to Gandhi in his last days.

In the political sphere Gandhi consistently stood by two principles: there could be no solution to the problem of the sub-continent until the British quit and there should be no partition. His anomalous position *vis-à-vis* the Congress Party remained: he was not even himself a 4-anna member and yet, with the leadership of the party still imprisoned, and despite his endless protestations that he spoke as an individual, Gandhi had to take on the role of Congress spokesman. He refused to withdraw the Quit India resolution and the authorities greeted a peaceful demonstration in Bombay on its anniversary, 9 August 1943, by arresting all 25 participating satyagrahis. Gandhi spoke of Congress readiness to jettison all plans for civil disobedience and to collaborate, should the government grant India immediate independence. A more meaningful dialogue was that between Gandhi and Jinnah during their talks at Jinnah's home in Bombay in September 1944. They met to discuss formulae drawn up by Rajagopalachari to overcome the communal impasse. He was the one outstanding (if in fact ex-Congress) leader still free and Gandhi welcomed his company, but in retrospect Rajagopalachari may have been unwise to steer Gandhi towards a dialogue with Jinnah which could only raise even higher the standing of the latter as the representative of Muslim interests.

With the Congress out of action after August 1942 a political vacuum developed which created space for the expanding influence of the Muslim League, and Gandhi confronted a Jinnah who was considerably more influential than in 1940. By 1945–6 the League was to gain control in both minority and majority Muslim areas. Jinnah had all the time to weigh the advantages of some offer of Muslim autonomy within a federal structure over his bid for an independent Pakistan: the Rajaji formula offered him a 'moth-eaten' Pakistan as he called it, for it entailed the division of Bengal and Punjab – he would have to accept that very partition in 1947. It also required him to accept independence first for a united India, before any independence would be granted to Pakistan, and this he flatly rejected. Gandhi grappled in vain with Jinnah's astute if narrow intelligence: 'I find no parallel in history', he stated, 'for a body of converts and their descendants claiming to be a nation apart from the parent stock. You seem to have introduced a new sort of nationhood' (quoted in Pyarelal 1956, p. 91).

The talks broke down on 27 September; they served only to further undermine Gandhi's standing as a man of political judgement in the eyes of the Congress. He had seemingly committed Congress to some form of partition. Circumstances surrounding the talks were ominous of the dangers to come: one of the Hindu Mahasabha pickets who had sought to frustrate Gandhi's departure for Bombay was his future assassin, N. V. Godse; while he was in Bombay, the paramilitary wing of the Muslim league, the Khaksars, paraded on the streets.

In some ways Gandhi became a marginal figure in the series of meetings and debates which led to the eventual reluctant acceptance by Congress of Viceroy Mountbatten's plan for independence of June 1947, which finally steered the sub-continent towards the setting up of two successor states to the Raj. It took time both for the British politicians and officials to recognize that power had passed to the real politicians of Congress, to Nehru and Patel, and for the Congress high command itself to acknowledge that Gandhi had become, in his own words, a 'back number'. With the break-up of the war-time coalition government in Britain the Conservatives sought some party solution to the Indian problem, and this led to Viceroy Wavell's Simla Conference of 25 June to 14 July 1945. This wretchedly broke down on Jinnah's insistence on caste–Hindu and Muslim parity in any putative interim government. Gandhi himself was perfectly happy to surrender any claims to Hindu equality provided the other minorities were fully represented. He told Wavell that he now saw himself as stepping into the shoes of Charles Andrews as an intermediary between India and the Raj (see p. 42).

The Labour general election victory promised real change, augured by the announcement on 15 March 1946 of a forthcoming Cabinet mission to India to try to draw up a settlement on the spot. Gandhi came to stay near the sweepers' (untouchables) bustee or slum colony in New Delhi, and then followed the mission up to Simla. With his old friend F. W. Pethick-Lawrence as Secretary of State for India and with Cripps convinced that Gandhi's negative attitude had sunk his mission in April 1942, particular attention was paid by the British to Gandhi's views, but in fact the newly released Congress high command was less and less ready to defer to Gandhi's judgement. Gandhi himself had profound reservations about the Cabinet mission's proposals: for a start, he believed nothing would work until the British had left India and that the mission itself must stick to its scheduled date of departure on 16 June. He believed that all interested parties – Hindus, Muslims, Sikhs – subconsciously believed that the British army would settle the outcome in their favour and this blocked any genuine effort at coming to an agreement. He also could not believe that a constituent assembly set up under the British would work. Although he could not formalize the nature of his fears, deep down he recognized an old Raj Machiavellian tactic of divide and rule at work. When he confronted the Congress working committee on 25 June 1946 he declared: 'I admit defeat. You are not bound to act upon my unsupported suspicions. You should follow my intuition only if it appeals to your reason. Otherwise take an independent course. I shall now leave with your permission. You should follow the dictates of your reason' (Pyarelal 1956, p. 228).

In fact, Nehru was already in part taking up Gandhi's point that the complicated recommendations on groupings, which conceded something of Jinnah's hopes for Pakistan, were voluntary and could not bind any future constituent assembly, but the high command no longer saw fit to listen to Gandhi's 'inner voice'; the time had come to work within the realities of power. The stakes were too high for any Gandhian experiment. It is now that, in Pyarelal's words, they dropped the pilot. Gandhi went on to defend their acceptance of the Cabinet mission at the AICC meeting on 7 July, but his central role in Congress policymaking was over. He played no part in the strange 'musical chairs' that ensued in the interim governments of 1946 nor in the elections for the constituent assembly. He was not sorry to see Wavell depart as Viceroy but his dealings with the new

Viceroy, Mountbatten, were minimal. He was preoccupied with the train of events unleashed by Jinnah, who, angry both at the Muslim League's failure to form the interim government on its own and at Nehru's seeming rejection of groupings, decided to declare 16 August 1946 as a Direct Action Day, a Muslim day of protest.

From that August day on into 1948 the length of the Gangetic plain, up into the North West Frontier Province, was ravaged by communal violence. The great Calcutta killings of 16–18 August were the catalyst. Muslim violence, officially sponsored by the Suhrawardy Muslim League government, was countered in Calcutta by Hindus; this spread to Muslim atrocities against the Hindu minority in Noakhali in Bengal (to become part of East Pakistan); the Hindus then struck back against the Muslim minority in Bihar. Violence also flared in the North West Frontier Province but the real bloodbath came in the Punjab. Gandhi made his heroic stance against communal violence in the east, in Noakhali, Bihar and Calcutta. (It has been perceptively described in N. K. Bose's memoir.) Gandhi had for some while wanted to visit Bengal to witness for himself the consequences of the severe famine of 1943: when he came, it was to witness another tragedy. Noakhali was to be the centre of his non-violence campaign from November 1946 until January 1947.

His priorities are revealing. He was not chiefly concerned with the loss of life and damage to property, and he was curiously tough-minded on refugees. He thought it monstrous they should accept mere hand-outs, echoing the old famine code of the Raj that refugees should receive aid only in return for work. His particular horror was forced conversion and his main concern for the Hindus was that they should be free to practise their religion. On the other hand, the Hindu minority in Noakhali were the wealthy and landowning class and he also took the acerbic view that perhaps this disaster would encourage them to start their lives over again on a higher plane, shedding their loyalties to caste and treating their subservient Muslim tenants with greater concern. His essential aim, however, was political, to probe the mind of the Muslim peasantry and find some way of bringing Muslim to live with Hindu and thus give the lie to Jinnah's two-nation theory. As partition loomed inescapably nearer, Gandhi was also ready to flirt with the plans of Suhrawardy, Chief Minister of Bengal and member of the Muslim League, but whose power-base was in Calcutta, whence his strong vested interest in maintaining an undivided Bengal, and Sarat Bose (Subhas's elder brother) for setting up an independent but united Bengal.

These cynical observations should not be allowed to overshadow the extraordinary moral struggle Gandhi conducted in the villages of East Bengal, mainly in his temporary ashram at Srirampur, trying by tireless propaganda and prayer to break down communal prejudice. But the Muslim peasantry did not want to listen: they told him that if he wished to display genuine impartiality, he should go to the aid of the Muslim minority in Bihar. This he did at the end of February 1947, and if here he was less the itinerant, basing himself in Patna and making visits to neighbouring villages, the same high moral purpose was pursued. He left Bihar on 30 March 1947. His extraordinary resistance to communalism was still not over: he came to Calcutta again to witness the moment of independence on 14 August, and undertook his penultimate fast, alongside a Muslim slum colony, on 1–4 September in a bid to stop a flaring up of communal violence in the city. Here his moral will prevailed, but the example was not strong enough to curb similar slaughter in the Punjab. He told people to accept the Mountbatten partition plan and the Boundary Award (drawn up at a very late stage by Sir Cyril Radcliffe), but, within, he recognized the failure of his vision of Swaraj.

There remained his dream of Ram Rajha. On leaving detention in 1944 he sensed the constructive programme had gone awry; it had failed to win Indians away from violence. One solution now was a radical reorganization. His vision was more and more anarchist, and he sought to decentralize the institutional structures of the constructive movement, weaken them as national institutions, and instead set up integrated bodies at village level, linking the Spinners Association, the Village Industries Association and the Hindustani Talimi Sangh (Basic Education Society). Single centres would thus be created, requiring a new type of all-round worker, concentrating the constructive movement at the village level and focusing on agriculture. The same ideas had inspired his confrontation with communalism, when he left a Congress worker in each village to tackle singlehanded the task of reconstruction. But Gandhi sensed a total reorientation was necessary: it was clear that the Congress Party had gone the way of power politics and would no longer be an instrument for the constructive movement. Perhaps the Congress should now liquidate itself as a party and a new movement should be fashioned to realize his ideals for village India. Perhaps, he began to wonder, Congress had never practised satyagraha as he understood it; perhaps it had never been more than the passive resistance of the weak.

He undertook his final fast against the communal madness on 13–17 January 1948. He was assassinated at a prayer meeting in the gardens of Birla House, New Delhi, on 30 January 1948. The shock of Gandhi's murder did something to abate the communal madness and there was huge relief when it was discovered that his assassin (N. V. Godse of the Hindu Mahasabha) was Hindu; the prospects of Hindu communal reprisals had it been a Muslim had been appalling. It was Gandhi's efforts to placate Muslim feelings by, for example, pleading for a generous financial settlement with the new state of Pakistan that had led to his being branded an appeaser and a traitor. His heroic stand against the tide of communalism had always carried with it the risk that he would become its victim.

7 The Legacy of Gandhi

Any discussion of Gandhi's legacy here can clearly be but a sketch. The longer-term impact of the man warrants a book in its own right. If all those individuals and movements that have been influenced by Gandhian ideals were to be listed it would read like a roll-call of the great moralists of the twentieth century, and of its great crusades. There is no scope here to discuss the careers of men like Danilo Dolci and Martin Luther King or the numerous civil rights campaigns and peace movements inspired by the ideal of passive disobedience and non-violence. Gandhi has inspired an opera, Philip Glass's *Satyagraha*, and novels, such as R. K. Narayan's *Waiting for the Mahatma*. Very briefly, the questions to be raised here will concern only the continuing influence and relevance of Gandhi's ideas to those two countries with which he was mainly concerned, India and South Africa.

It is often assumed that within India Gandhi suffered the fate of all political saints – he was placed on a pedestal and forgotten. This is untrue. The ideas of Gandhi continued to be debated among Gandhians, his opponents, especially the Indian Communists, and the ruling elite, particularly during the prime ministership of Jawaharlal Nehru. Vinoba Bhave, Gandhi's heir-apparent, took over the Gandhian constructive movement, giving it a more radical edge through his attempt, in the Bhoodan movement, to bring about a voluntary redistribution of land to the poorer peasantry, above all, to the landless. He was to be strongly supported by Jayaprakash Narayan, whose socialism took on an increasingly Gandhian complexion, and who began to devise sophisticated programmes for the modernization of Indian villages but still inspired by a Gandhian anarchist vision of decentralization and self-sufficiency. Narayan, or J.P., as he was familiarly known, exerted enormous moral influence by the 1970s and became the leader of national opposition to Prime Minister Indira Gandhi (Nehru's daughter, no relation of the Mahatma) during the Emergency period of 1975–7. His leadership does much to explain the astonishing defeat of the Congress Party in the 1979 elections.

The Bhoodan movement arose in response to the Communist inspired Telengana revolution in southern India in the late 1940s and a case can be made for seeing the Gandhian movement as a conscious response to the challenge of Communism. Certainly the Indian Communist movement saw in Gandhism a rival to its expansion, and this could find unusually bitter expression, as is shown by the vandalism of statues of Gandhi by young people inspired by the extreme left wing Naxalite movement. Yet some Communists, e.g. P. C. Joshi, were well aware that Gandhi had made an impact on the Indian people in ways that the Communist movement had failed to do and that they had much to learn from the nature of Gandhi's appeal to the peasantry (see in particular P. C. Joshi's essay in K. N. Panikkar, 1980).

The impact of Gandhi's ideas on government policy is even more striking. Indian manufacture remained subject to Gandhian practice to an extraordinary extent. The hand-loom textile industry in 1968 was producing 45 per cent of cloth output. In total, small-scale enterprise continued to produce 40 per cent of all output and employ three-quarters of the labour force. One commentator has characterized the successive five-year economic plans as 'a curious amalgam of Stalinist and Ruskinian views' (Madison, 1971).

Attempts to inject Gandhian ideals through the village uplift programme, or Panchayat Raj, were less successful, but are further proof of Nehru's continuing deference to Gandhi's beliefs. There is even the fascinating possibility, in a quite different sphere of policy, that Nehru was inspired by the satyagraha ideals of non-violence in his response to the Chinese invasion of 1962, and that the confrontation between poorly armed and clad Indian troops and the Chinese in Aksai Chin was the belated indication of how Indians would have confronted the Japanese in 1942 (Maxwell, 1972). Yet the continuing plight of the untouchables and of women in India (one notices in particular repressive caste communal conflicts in Ahmedabad in 1985) point to the limited success of Gandhi's ideals in terms of social change.

Gandhi's South African legacy introduces two themes: the fate of the South African Indians and the debate on whether to pursue a non-violent or violent strategy against apartheid. The second aspect has to be placed in the wider context of the character of freedom or liberation struggles within the Third World.

Gandhi's career began in South Africa as an assimilationist and ended in India as a nationalist. He always displayed anger towards colonial-born Indians who disparaged India and its culture. He gave little guidance as to how South African Indians might best relate in the long run to the society in which they found themselves. In fact, after 1917, despite the constraints on occupation and residence of the emerging apartheid system, they were to modernize. With the phasing out of indentured labour, Indians were in time to leave the sugar plantations and coalfields. Between 1911 and 1946, as a percentage of the labour force, on the former they dropped from 88 to 7 per cent, on the latter, from 40 to 3 per cent. Where free to do so, immigrant Indian communities turn to trade and commerce, and in South Africa they did become an increasingly urbanized community, above all in Durban. But such integration was often in the face of governmental and social resistance and Indians found themselves confronting very difficult questions of political strategy.

All the while apartheid was strengthening: Indians suffered restrictions in employment introduced by the 1926 Apprenticeship Act; constraints on residence, if in fact resolved voluntarily, came close to anticipating the Group Areas Act of 1950, one of the most iniquitous measures introduced by the Nationalists after they came to power in 1948. The crisis came with the introduction under a Smuts government in 1946 of the Asiatic Land Tenure and Indian Representatives Bill, the so-called Ghetto Act. The Indian National Congress in South Africa had at first fallen apart on Gandhi's departure but it eventually came together again, initially under the leadership of a Durban-based merchant, A. I. Kajee. This was leadership by the 'passenger' elite. By the 1940s, however, power had passed to the ex-indentured Indians, to Tamils rather than Gujarati, to lower castes, and this bred a more radical approach. In 1946, in response to the Act, the Indians took up satyagraha for the first time since Gandhi's departure. Gandhi was delighted. Clearly he had now grasped more of the realities of South Africa, for his advice to the South African Indians was to form a common anti-white front, but he warned them of the need to train blacks in the ways of satyagraha.

The Ghetto Act was, for a while, delayed. Gandhi's warning, however, was all too quickly borne out by the Durban riots of

101

1949. When a young Zulu attacked an Indian shop assistant, he retaliated. Blacks turned on Indians and in the ensuing violence 147 people were killed and 1,078 injured. When the blacks, at the bottom of the economic pile, came up against more prosperous Indians, often running the buses which took them in to Durban from their shanty towns or acting as rack-renting landlords, African–Asian communal violence was the consequence. South African Indians were now forced to consider where they stood on the question of apartheid.

Gandhian-style resistance to apartheid was part of the wider struggle against colonialism and neo-colonialism. With India being the first colonial society to acquire independence, it was inevitable that Gandhi's method should be keenly studied within the Third World and, as Nehru became increasingly important in international affairs as the moving spirit behind the Non-Aligned Movement (i.e. those countries not aligned to either of the great East–West superpowers), India's example became all the more influential. Nkrumah, for example, was seemingly to adopt Gandhian methods in leading the Gold Coast (Ghana) to independence by 1957. But critics began to wonder, as the newly independent states failed to introduce radical policies and remained seemingly dependent on former metropolitan states, whether something was not fundamentally wrong with the Gandhian approach, and a strident new voice was heard in the writings of the West Indian psychiatrist, Frantz Fanon, who was to devote his life to the Algerian freedom struggle, arguing a case for the necessity of violence to exorcise the trauma of colonialism and to drive the neo-colonialist bourgeoisie forward into revolutionary alliance with the peasantry.

Echoes of this debate have haunted the liberation struggle in South Africa. Under the dynamic leadership of a new generation of Africans – Walter Sisulu, Oliver Tambo and Nelson Mandela – the African National Congress became a far more potent force in politics. Their initial line, revealed in the Defiance Campaign of 1952 and in the Kliptown African Freedom Charter of 1955, under the moral guidance of Chief Albert Luthuli, was for a Gandhian-style civil rights movement, but the ANC was subject to profound tensions and this led, on the one hand, in 1959, to the breakaway of the PAC (Pan-African Congress) – more populist, more peasant-based, more Africanist and less multi-racial in its approach – and on the other, to the decision by Nelson Mandela to go for armed struggle, with the setting up of the Umkhonto We Sizwe (Spear of the Nation) on 16 December 1961. Maybe the massacre at Sharpeville in March 1960 played the same role in radicalizing ANC strategies as had the events at Amritsar for the Indian Congress.

Gandhi would no doubt have advocated the continuing alliance of South African Indians with anti-apartheid forces. He would have deplored both the readiness of Indians to advance the interests of Indian capitalism within the permitted limits of apartheid and Indian collaboration with the recent tricameral political system introduced by the Nationalist regime. But Gandhi would have vigorously rejected recourse to terrorism, above all against persons, but also against property (only the second has been officially sanctioned by the ANC in exile). The thrust of this book has suggested, however, that Gandhi would have been far more sympathetic to outbreaks of 'spontaneous' resistance to apartheid, even if such outbreaks spilled over into attacks on property, and that in Gandhi's scheme of things there would have been a parallel to draw between the Quit India rebellion of 1942 and the Soweto uprising of 1976. But one cannot be certain of this. Because Gandhi reacted so concretely to each distinct challenge, there always remains an area of imprecision about where he stood on some basic issues of strategy. The debate on the role of violence continues.

Gandhi was a world historical figure. It has not been enough to assess him by his own standards and ambitions; he has become part of twentieth-century history and his impact has to be measured as much by the consequences of his actions as by his intentions. This short study of Gandhi has stressed a historically contextual rather than a biographical approach. Gandhi has been seen through the eyes of his contemporaries, as someone caught up in the ebb and flow of events, sometimes taking a central role, sometimes on the periphery. It is an approach that, while emphasizing Gandhi's role as a catalyst to events, has also drawn attention to the shortcomings of his actions, to the way they deflected or even disregarded alternative solutions to problems.

To recognize the universality of Gandhi's ideas is to acknowledge his greatness, but there was also an elusive open-endedness in his values and ambitions. All kinds of interpreters can harness something of Gandhi's philosophy to argue this or that case, this or that solution to economic, social and political problems. But Gandhi's place in history is too important to allow him to disappear behind a smokescreen of interpretations. Accordingly, this study of his life and thought has aimed to provide a clear introduction to his views, attitudes and historical role.

Glossary

Adivasi	Member of the untouchable caste.
Ahimsa	Non-injury, non-violence.
Arya Samaj	A Hindu reform movement founded by Dayanand Saraswati in 1875.
Ashram	A spiritual retreat: centres of Gandhi's constructive movement.
Bania	Member of the merchant caste.
Bhakti	Devotion, worship.
Bhoodan	Voluntary gift of land for the landless: a Gandhian movement led by Vinoba Bhave.
Brahmacharya	One of the Hindu stages of life: a vow of celibacy.
Brahmin	Member of the priestly caste.
Chitpavin	A category of the Brahmin caste in Western India.
Dharma	Customary observance, duty, law: the underlying social morality of Hinduism.
Dhoti	Loin cloth; the traditional dress of the Indian peasant.
Diarchy	Dual rule, as practised under the Montagu–Chelmsford reforms, 1918–35.
Hartal	A form of strike.
Jain, Jainism	A religion noted for its emphasis on non-injury, or ahimsa, particularly strong in Western India.
Jajmani	Division of labour and a system of social interdependence within the hierarchical Hindu caste structure.
Jati	Birth, caste.
Kali Yuga	The last and worst of the four ages in the Hindu cycle – the Black Age.
Khadi	Hand-spun cloth; a major part of Gandhi's economic reform programme.
Khilafat	Post First World War Muslim movement to protect the Sultan of Turkey, spiritual ruler or Caliph (Khalifa) of Islam.

Kshatriya	Member of the warrior or kingly caste.
Mahatma	Literally great soul: title first conferred on Gandhi by Rabindranath Tagore, friend of Gandhi and a writer and educationalist.
Mantra	A mystical verse or magical formula.
Maulana	Title of respect given to Muslim men of learning.
Marwari	Rich merchant caste, originally from Rajasthan.
Mofussil	Country or provincial area as opposed to a city.
Moplah	Muslim peasantry in Malabar.
Panchayat	A court of arbitration.
Panchayat Raj	A form of village democracy.
Ram Rajha	Kingdom of God or Righteousness on Earth.
Ramayana	Hindu classic describing Rama's struggle with Ravana.
Sabha	Assembly, association.
Saivite	Hindu sect worshipping Siva, the destroyer god.
Sanatanist	Orthodox Hindu.
Sanyassin	A wandering recluse: a holy man.
Satya	Truth.
Sarvodaya	The welfare or rise of all, social uplift: Gandhi's social philosophy.
Satyagraha	Truth-force: Gandhi's technique of passive, non-violent, resistance.
Shuddi	Hindu reconversion movement.
Sudra	Member of the labourer castes, often a peasant.
Swadeshi	Literally, produced in one's own country: a programme of economic self-reliance.
Swaraj	Self-rule.
Taluq	Sub-division of a district.
Taluqdar	Title of landowner, particularly in the United Provinces.
Tapas	Ascetic practices.
Ulama	Muslim priests.
Vaishnavite	Hindu sect worshipping Vishnu, the preserver god.
Varna	Literally colour: the four classes of men; less accurately, another term for the four main castes.
Vedas	The sacred texts of early Hinduism.
Vedantin	Philosophical tradition based on these texts.

References and Further Reading

The asterisk denotes works that are particularly useful for students.

Andrews, C. F. (ed.) 1930: *Mahatma Gandhi: His Own Story*. London.
*Ashe, G. 1968: *Gandhi: A Study in Revolution*. London.
Azad, Maulana 1959: *India Wins Freedom*. Calcutta.
Basham, A. L. 1954: *The Wonder that was India*. London.
Baker, C. et al. (ed.) 1981: *Power, Profits and Politics*. Cambridge.
Behn, Mira (Madeleine Slade) 1960: *The Spirit's Pilgrimage*. London.
Birkenhead, F. W. F. S. 1965: *The Life of Lord Halifax*. London.
Bose, Mihir 1982: *The Lost Hero: A Biography of Subas Bose*. London.
Bose, N. K. 1953: *My Days with Gandhi*. Delhi.
Bose, Subas Chandra 1948: *The Indian Struggle*. Calcutta.
Bradnock, R. W. 1984: *Agricultural Change in South Asia*. London.
*Brown, Judith M. 1972: *Gandhi's Rise to Power: Indian Politics 1915–1922*. Cambridge.
Brown, Judith M. 1977: *Gandhi and Civil Disobedience: The Mahatma in Indian Politics, 1928–1934*. Cambridge.
Brown, Judith M. 1985: *Modern India: the Origins of an Asian Democracy*. Oxford.
Caute, D. 1970: *Fanon*. London.
Chandra, Bipan 1966: *The Rise and Growth of Economic Nationalism in India*. New Delhi.
Charlesworth, N. 1982a: *British Rule and the Indian Economy 1800–1914*. London.
Charlesworth, N. 1982b: 'Themes and Problems in Indian Economic History 1914–1939'. *South Asia Research*, vol. 2, pp. 23–33.
*Chatterjee, Margaret 1983: *Gandhi's Religious Thought*. London.
*Cohn, B. S. 1971: *India: the Social Anthropology of a Civilisation*. Englewood Cliffs, New Jersey.
Copley, A. R. H. 1978: *The Political Career of C. Rajagopalachari: A Moralist in Politics 1937–1954*. New Delhi.
Copley, A. R. H. 1986: *C. Rajagopalachari: Gandhi's Southern Commander*. Madras.

Cronin, R. 1985: 'Quite quiet Indian: the despair of R. K. Narayan'. *Encounter*, vol. 64, pp. 52–9.

Desai, A. R. 1948: *The Social Background of Indian Nationalism*. Bombay.

*Desai, A. R. (ed.) 1979: *Peasant Struggles in India*. New Delhi.

Devanesan, Chandran D. S. 1969: *The Making of the Mahatma*. Madras.

Dumont, L. 1972: *Homo Hierarchichus*. London.

Erikson, Erik H. 1970: *Gandhi's Truth*. London.

Fischer, Louis 1951: *The Life of Mahatma Gandhi*. London.

Furneaux, R. 1963: *Massacre at Amritsar*. London.

Gallagher, J., Johnson, G. and Seal, A. (eds) 1973: *Locality, Province, Nation*. Cambridge.

Gandhi, M. K. 1927: *An Autobiography or The Story of My Experiments with Truth*. Ahmedabad.

Gandhi, M. K. 1963: *Hind Swaraj* (first published 1909) in *The Collected Works*, vol. X. Ahmedabad. (The first volume was published in 1958 and the collection is not yet complete.)

Ghosh, Sudhir 1967: *Gandhi's Emissary*. London.

Glendevon, J. 1971: *The Viceroy at Bay*. London.

Gopal, S. 1957: *The Viceroyalty of Lord Irwin*. Oxford.

Gopal, S. 1975: *Jawaharlal Nehru. A Biography*, vol. I 1889–1947. London.

Gordon, L. 1974: *Bengal: the Nationalist Movement 1876–1940*. New York.

Grigg, J. 1983: 'Recessional or progressional: after empire'. *Encounter*, vol. 61.

*Guha, Ranajit (ed.) 1982/83: *Subaltern Studies*, vol. I/II. *Writings in South Asian History and Society*. Delhi.

Hancock, W. N. 1962: *Smuts: the Sanguine Years*, vol. I 1870–1919. Cambridge.

*Hardiman, D. 1981: *Peasant Nationalists of Gujarat: Kheda District 1917–1934*. New Delhi.

*Hardy, P. 1972: *The Muslims of British India*. Cambridge.

Hobsbawn, E. J. et al. 1980: *Peasants in History*. Calcutta.

Hunt, J. D. 1978: *Gandhi in London*. New Delhi.

*Hutchins, F. G. 1973: *India's Revolution: Gandhi and the Quit India Movement*. Cambridge, Mass.

*Iyer, Raghavan 1973: *The Moral and Political Thought of Mahatma Gandhi*. Oxford.

Johnson, G. 1973: *Provincial Politics and Indian Nationalism: Bombay and the Indian National Congress 1880–1915*. Cambridge.

Johnson, G. 1984: 'Gandhi's politics'. *The Cambridge Review*, July, pp. 135–40.

Keer, Dhananjay 1966: *Veer Savarkar*. Bombay.

Keer, Dhananjay 1971: *Ambedkar: Life and Mission*. Bombay.

Kumar, Ravinder (ed.) 1971: *Essays on Gandhian Politics: the Rowlatt Satyagraha*. Oxford.

Lannoy, R. 1971: *The Speaking Tree*. Oxford.

Lynch, O. 1969: *The Politics of Untouchability*. Chicago.

McClane, John P. 1971: *Indian Nationalism and the Early Congress*. Princeton, New Jersey.

*McPherson, K. 1980: *Jinnah*. Sydney.

Maddison, A. 1971: *Class Structures and Economic Growth: India and Pakistan since the Moghuls*. London.

Mandelbaum, D. G. 1970: *Society in India*, vols I and II. Berkeley, California.

Markovits, C. 1981: 'Indian business and the Congress provincial governments 1937–1939'. *Modern Asian Studies*, 15, pp. 487–526.

Mascaro, J. (trans.) 1962: *The Bhagavad Gita* (Penguin Classics edn). Harmondsworth.

Maxwell, N. 1972: *India's China War*. London.

Mehta, V. 1977: *Mahatma Gandhi and his Apostles*. New York.

*Minault, Gail 1982: *The Khilafat Movement*. New York.

Moore, Barrington Jnr 1966: *Social Origins of Dictatorship and Democracy*. New York.

Moore, R. J. 1974: *The Crisis of Indian Unity 1917–1940*. Oxford.

Moore, R. J. 1979: *Churchill, Cripps and India 1939–1945*. Oxford.

Moore, R. J. 1983: *Escape from Empire; The Attlee Government and the Indian Problem* (Oxford).

Nanda, B. R. 1958: *Mahatma Gandhi: A Biography*. London.

*Nanda, B. R. et al. *Gandhi and Nehru*. New Delhi.

Nandy, Ashis 1983: *The Intimate Enemy*. Delhi.

Nehru, Jawaharlal 1936: *Towards Freedom: An Autobiography*. London.

Ostergaard, G. and Currell, M. 1971: *The Gentle Anarchists*. Oxford.

Pandey, B. N. 1969: *The Break-up of British India*. London.

Pandey, B. N. 1976: *Nehru*. London.

*Pandey, Gyanendra 1978: *The Ascendancy of the Congress in Uttar Pradesh 1926–1934*. New Delhi.

*Panikkar, K. N. (ed.) 1980: *National and Left Movements in India*. New Delhi.

Philips, C. H. (ed.) 1962: *The Evolution of India and Pakistan*. Oxford.

Prasad, Bimal (ed.) 1980: *A Revolutionary's Quest: Selected Writings of Jayaprakash Narayan*. New Delhi.

Pyarelal (Pyarelal Nayar) 1956: *Mahatma Gandhi: the last Phase*, vols I and II. Ahmedabad.

Pyarelal (Pyarelal Nayar) 1980: *Mahatma Gandhi*, vol. II *The Discovery of Satyagraha – on the Threshold*. Bombay.

Rao, B. Shiva 1939: *The Industrial Worker in India*. London.

Ray, Rajat K. 1979: *Industrialisation in India*. New Delhi.

Raychaudhuri, Tapan 1979: 'Indian nationalism as animal politics'. *Historical Journal*, vol. 22, pp. 747–63.

Rizvi, Gowher 1984: 'The Congress revolt of 1942: a reassessment'. *Indo–British Review: A Journal of History*, vol. 11, pp. 28–45.

Rothermund, I. 1963: *The Philosophy of Restraint*. Bombay.

Rudolph, L. I. and Rudolph, S. H. 1967: *The Modernity of Tradition*. Chicago.

Rudolph, L. I. and Rudolph, S. H. 1983: *Gandhi: the Traditional Roots of Charisma*. London and Chicago.

Runyan, W. M. 1984: *Life Histories and Psychobiography*. New York.

Seal, A. 1968: *The Emergence of Indian Nationalism*. Cambridge.

Sitaramayya, Pattabhi 1947/1969: *History of the Indian National Congress*, vol. I/II. Bombay.

Smuts, J. C. 1952: *Jan Christian Smuts*. London.

Spear, P. 1965: *The Oxford History of Modern India 1740–1947*. Oxford.

Smith, W. Cantwell 1943: *Modern Islam in India*. Lahore.

Srinivas, M. N. 1968: *Social Change in Modern India*. Berkeley, California.

Tahmankar, D. V. 1970: *Sardar Patel*. London.

Tinker, H. 1974: *A New System of Slavery: the Export of Indian Labour Overseas 1830–1920*. London.

Tinker, H. 1976: *Separate and Unequal: India and the Indians in the Commonwealth*. London.

Tinker, H. 1977: *The Banyan Tree: Overseas Emigrants from India, Pakistan and Bangladesh*. Oxford.

Tinker, H. 1979: *The Ordeal of Love: C. F. Andrews and India*. New Delhi.

Thursby, G. R. 1975: *Hindu–Muslim Relations in British India*. Leiden.

Tomlinson, B. R. 1979: *The Political Economy of the Raj 1914–47*. Cambridge.

Troup, F. 1972: *South Africa: A Historical Introduction*. London.

Van Onselen, C. 1982: *Studies in the Social and Economic History of the Witwatersrand 1886–1914*. Vol. I, *New Babylon*: vol. II, *New Nineveh*. Johannesburg.

Woodcock, G. 1972: *Gandhi*. London.

Woodruff, P. 1953: *The Men Who Ruled India*, vol. II. London.

Index

117

Index by Meg Davies